Lee Sandlin

DISTANCERS

Lee Sandlin is the author of *Wicked River: The Missis-sippi When It Last Ran Wild* and reviews books for *The Wall Street Journal.* His essay "Losing the War" was included in the anthology *The New Kings of Nonfic-tion.* He lives in Chicago.

DISTANCERS

AN AMERICAN MEMOIR

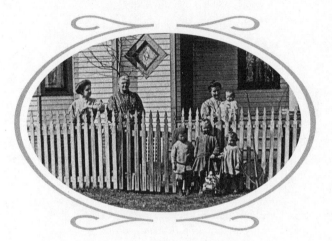

Lee Sandlin

Vintage Books

A Division of Random House, Inc. | *New York*

A VINTAGE ORIGINAL, JULY 2013

Copyright © 2004, 2013 by Lee Sandlin

All rights reserved. Published in the United States
by Vintage Books, a division of Random House, Inc., New York, and
in Canada by Random House of Canada Limited, Toronto.

Vintage and colophon are registered trademarks of Random House, Inc.

This work was originally serialized, in slightly different form,
in the *Chicago Reader*, in 2004.

Library of Congress Cataloging-in-Publication Data:
Sandlin, Lee.
The distancers : an American memoir / Lee Sandlin.
pages   cm.
ISBN 978-0-345-80676-5 (alk. paper)
1. Sandlin, Lee.   2. Sandlin, Lee—Family.
3. German Americans—Middle West—Biography.
4. Middle West—Social Life and customs.
5. Middle West—Biography.   I. Title.
CT275.S2584A3 2013
920.00977—dc23
[B]   2013011901

Book design by Heather Kelly

www.vintagebooks.com

Printed in the United States of America.
10 9 8 7 6 5 4 3 2 1

FOR ALISON TRUE

sed tua me virtus tamen et sperata voluptas
suavis amicitiae quemvis sufferre laborem
suadet et inducit noctes vigilare serenas

Though for no other cause, yet for this: that posterity may know we have not loosely through silence permitted things to pass away as in a dream.

—RICHARD HOOKER,
Of the Laws of Ecclesiastical Polity (1594)

Contents

Prologue   xi

1

Just Shy of the Mississippi   3

2

Bosh's Only Idea   19

3

The Last of the Old Country   35

4

The Champion Distancer   51

5

We Can't Take Care of Our Own   67

6

The World Doesn't Owe You a Living   81

Contents

7

War Fever 95

8

Nobody Would Ever Guess 111

9

One Last Parade 131

10

Things They Never Told 145

11

This Is All I Know 167

Afterword: Heilongjiang 183

Acknowledgments and Thanks 195

Prologue

IN DOWNSTATE ILLINOIS near the Mississippi River, there was an old house that belonged to my family. It was a small clapboard house built in the classic heartland style, with a big yard, lush gardens, and the inevitable white picket fence out front. It stood on the outskirts of Edwardsville, right where the last streets gave way to open countryside. It was a beautiful place. When you looked out from the porch on a summer's day, you had an unbroken view of meadows and fields and remote blue hills shimmering in the golden heat. You'd swear that nothing had ever happened there more dramatic than a passing thunderstorm.

The house played a big role in my family history. My great-grandfather built it at the turn of the last century; my grandfather grew up there, and it's where my mother spent her summers when she was a kid. By the time of my childhood it had been firmly established as a kind of private sleepaway camp for our family. As soon as school let out for the year, our parents would take us from the Chicago suburbs to Edwardsville, where they'd leave us for weeks or sometimes months at a time. One of my cousins claims there was a year when her parents didn't come back for her until Christmas.

I can't remember how often I stayed there myself, or how long those stays lasted; they've all blurred together into a kind of eternal Tom Sawyer–ish reverie. Back then Edwardsville was a postcard-perfect Midwestern town, a place of towering shade trees and well-tended hedges, placid side streets and meandering back alleys. It was an ideal setting for childhood adventures. It was where I graduated from a tricycle to a bicycle, and from softball to hardball; the first tree I ever climbed solo was a weeping willow by the picket fence, and I still remember finding a cicada shell stuck to a branch at its heart, like a statuette of Martian jade.

But mainly what I remember about the house is its gardens. They were mazes of flower beds that filled up most of the enormous backyard; each year that I visited, they'd spread farther around the side of the house and out toward the street. The few times I dared to venture alone into their interior, I was immediately lost in a disorienting riot of brilliant colors and intoxicating smells. There were endless beds of red and yellow tulips, bristling stands of zinnias and asters and snapdragons, towering skylines of gladioli and sunflowers, fog banks of Queen Anne's lace, and rose trellises as intricate as fireworks. And then there were the bumblebees. They floated down every path—swarming in the long sunlit aisles, hovering and drifting and clustering and swerving from blossom to blossom like commuters in an aerial city. That was a heady sight for a suburban kid like me, who'd been taught to think of all insects as rare and threatening invaders.

But then there were always lessons at the house. It was really a boot camp in what are now called old-fashioned values. Our four hosts—my great-aunts Hilda and Helen and my great-uncles Marty and Eugene—made it plain to us that everything said and done and thought there was swathed in morality and custom. We learned the proper way to be deferential to our elders, the proper way of washing our hands before meals (the soap was scratchy and smelled of coconut), the proper way of saying prayers at bedtime (on your knees, out loud, hands folded on the bedspread, an adult auditor present). There was a proper way to say please and thank you at the dinner table, and, more crucially, a proper time to say them—the airspace above the table was as crowded as O'Hare, and a wrongly calculated grab at a bowl or pitcher or platter as it passed from hand to hand could cause a disastrous midair collision.

Edwardsville was the first place where I understood what manners were for. Back home they made no sense; they seemed to be nothing more than a bunch of meaningless gestures parents foisted on kids to test their obedience. But here they were unobtrusively essential. They allowed people who may not have even liked one another much to get along effortlessly in the closest quarters. They were a way for tradition, faith, courtesy, and habit to exchange places in a ceaseless dance.

At the heart of these lessons was Sunday morning at church. This was the most essential ritual, and it was the only one I never quite mastered. You had to be awake, scrubbed raw, crammed into your best clothes, and lined up on the front porch before the church bells started tolling. No matter how early I started, I was always late. By the time I reached the porch, with soap still sticky behind my ears and my shirt buttoned wrong, the whole neighborhood had already come streaming past—girls in white blouses and billowy pastel skirts, boys in white shirts and long pants and strangle-knotted ties, men in ancient, spotless suits, and women in brilliant dresses emblazoned with storms of birds and flowers. Sometimes, when we were all hurrying down the now deserted street as though late for the ark, the bells were already falling silent. Sometimes we were racing against a morning thunderstorm swelling up in the high summer heat, so that as we overtook the last stragglers, we found the steeple in dazzling white starkness against the black western sky, standing tall like a rebuke to the turbulence of the trees.

Inside, the air was suffocatingly sultry and the pews were hard. People sighed and rustled and coughed; they fanned themselves furiously and glared daggers at their neighbors as though blaming them for the heat. The minister stood at a plain pulpit of varnished blond wood before a big window of

clear glass. He spoke softly but forcefully about the imma-
nence of God in the world around us and the dire certainty
of His approaching judgment. Sometimes the storm broke
over the church as he spoke, and his words were drowned out
by the wild drumming of rain on the glass—but he never
acknowledged the fury around him even by so much as raising
his voice. Then the black clouds behind him would unravel,
and the sunlight would come pouring through the window in
furnace-hot shafts; and as my suit dissolved into scratchy ooze
and the hymnals burned to the touch, I understood what it felt
like to be caught in the crosshairs of God.

Our hosts were really the best possible exemplars of this
way of life. The four were all around sixty when I first stayed
with them, and to me that was as old as Methuselah. Their
hair was white, their faces had tectonic wrinkles, and the
touch of their skin was dinosaur leathery. But their laughter
bubbled out of them in a ceaseless froth, as though welling up
from a hidden spring. To this day, whenever I think of them,
I remember that sound: Hilda's bright trill, Helen's wheezy,
half-smothered chortle, Marty's haw-haw bray, and Eugene's
rare, lone snort like a stone dropped in a well. It was a kind
of laughter that radiated well-being, acceptance, faith. Just
being around it made you exhilarated, even when you were the
target.

And you could be certain you would be the target, sooner
or later. The four of them were brutal about everything they
didn't like, and the main thing they didn't like was the world

outside Edwardsville. That included us. They thought we were citified, willful, too big for our britches, forever putting on airs. When I had to start wearing glasses, they spent that entire summer, with ever-replenished hilarity, calling me "Four-eyes." Once one of my cousins staged a play she'd written, with the rest of the kids as actors, and our hosts broke it up by standing in unison and booing and hissing and pelting us with wadded-up Kleenex until the author ran off in tears.

In a way, that was their real lesson—reticence. All their instruction in correct behavior, in modesty and practicality and self-reliance and respect, really came down to this: there is never a good time to talk about yourself. Your problems are nobody's business. Your triumphs are nothing special. Never boast, never complain, never reveal, never admit, never take pride, never expect a compliment, never look for sympathy or commiseration or approval. The only thing more offensive than asking a personal question is answering one; the most important goal in life is to keep your distance.

There were moments when they succeeded too well. It sometimes happened in the evenings, as we sat around the big dining table. Everything would just stop. The deck of cards would lie unshuffled; the conversation would dry up; the laughter would die away like a sweet breeze in the summer heat. Our four hosts would sit motionless, their heads bowed, staring fiercely at the floor. I learned better than to say anything then; any attempt to lighten the mood would be met with glares of hostility and incomprehension. There was absolutely nothing to be said; no thought was impersonal enough; no emotion that wouldn't be in bad taste. As the silence deepened I'd feel as though they were fossilizing before my eyes: those Germanic peasant foreheads, those round cheeks, those hatchet noses, those glinting, heavy-lidded, suspicious eyes—they were like stone trolls in a forest glen.

That was when I was most acutely aware of how little I really understood about them. In all the years I'd been coming there, I'd never heard them say a word about their past. They never gossiped or reminisced; by the time of my last stay, when I was twelve, I still didn't know the first thing about their lives. Why were they all sharing the house? How exactly were they even related to one another—were they all siblings, two married couples, what? And why, if they loved children so much, did none of them have children of their own? I didn't know, and nobody would explain it to me. It was as though they'd already slipped out of reach.

It was only during that last summer that I got up the nerve to pry. I approached Helen, the one I always thought of as the nicest of the four. I don't remember my exact question; it was something like, "Have you all always lived here together?"

The effect on her was astonishing. She seemed to rear up and exhale flame, like a startled basilisk. "In my day," she gasped out, "people didn't talk about themselves." She eyed me with annihilating contempt. "And *especially* not to the children."

Today there's nothing left of the family in Edwardsville. My relatives are scattered around the heartland and the Pacific Northwest—steady suburban home owners for the most part, churchgoing Republicans, devotees of skiing and stomach stapling and SUVs. But they still talk about the house sometimes. The talk is invariably affectionate, even devoted. The house was, one of my cousins said to me recently, "a place where anyone could feel truly loved."

But they also think its part in the family story is long over with, and they aren't interested in preserving its memory. A few years ago, when the question came up of what to do with the property, the word went around that anybody in the family who wanted it could move in rent free. There were no takers. The house was fine as a daydream, but nobody actually wanted to live there. On the other hand, there wasn't much enthusiasm about selling it, either. One of my aunts told me she wanted the house demolished. We were done with it now, and she'd rather see it gone than occupied by strangers.

I'm sure that's a sentiment the house's inhabitants would have understood. They didn't mean to leave anything of themselves behind. No colorful anecdotes, no fond memories, no diaries: only a handful of letters and a thin scattering of mementos. This is the way things have always gone in my family. Most of my ancestors deliberately lived without drama, without attracting the slightest notice from the outside world, as though being visible were no different from being immoral. They all wanted to pass through their lives unobserved by anyone but God.

As far as my relatives today are concerned, that's just the way it should be. For them, the story of the old family house is simple. The people who lived there were happy—more than happy: their lives were steeped in a kind of sweetness that we can only envy now. And maybe that's true. At least, the history of the household, as far as I've been able to reconstruct it, really was remarkably placid and unruffled for quite a long while. But I keep remembering a conversation I had with an old family friend, somebody who'd known several generations of the Edwardsville house, all the way back to my great-grandfather. I asked her, "Do you think they were happy?"

I was half expecting her to dismiss my impertinence with a thunderclap of rage, the way Helen once had. Instead, she thought for a long while. Then she emitted a slow sigh.

"I suppose one or two of them might have been happy, in their way," she said. "But they sure were good at hiding it."

The
DISTANCERS

1

Just Shy of the Mississippi

MY GREAT-GREAT-GREAT-GRANDPARENTS Peter and Elizabeth Sehnert came to America from Germany around 1850. They had no friends or family waiting for them when their ship landed, and they knew absolutely nothing about the New World. So they used a simple method to find a home. They rode the trains inland as far as the trains could go.

It took them more than a week. They traveled in swaying monotony from the industrialized cities of the Northeast through the newly cleared farmlands of Ohio and Indiana. Only west of Chicago did the settlements thin out and the landscape start to look almost pristine. The train service out there was sporadic and the cars were almost always empty. People said you could ride a train through Illinois from sunup to sundown and not see another living soul except the conductor.

The Sehnerts reached the end of the line at a country station just shy of the Mississippi River. They could have kept going; a lot of people did. Those were the years of the Gold Rush and the great westward migration: as fast as new settlers were arriving in Illinois, the old ones were packing up, selling out, and heading west to California. There weren't any bridges yet across the Mississippi, and there were so many people, wagons, and animals piling up at the ferry points that the wait for a crossing sometimes lasted for days.

But the Sehnerts weren't tempted. The journey west was overland through Kansas, or by steamship up the Missouri, through a dangerous country that seemed to be over the edge of the world. So they stayed on what they thought of as the civilized side of the river. They bought a small farm in the open country near Greenville, Illinois.

The name Sehnert is an old one. It goes back deep into the Middle Ages and the ancient farming communities along the Rhine. (It has an archaic and peculiar sound even to a lot of Germans, who tend to think it's a misprint of Schnert.) Peter and Elizabeth arrived in America with the vast weight of their ancestral values still intact. They were humble, God-fearing, churchgoing, intensely taciturn people; they would no more complain about their lot in life than they would ask a neighbor for help in an emergency.

But there was one way in which they couldn't help but stand out: they were Catholic.

The heartland in those days was thinly settled but thick with eccentricity. It was a world of ranters, fire-tongued preachers, Pentecostalists, snake handlers, and river baptizers; and the tide of new immigration from Germany was bringing in a florid assortment of socialists, Freemasons, Fourierists, labor agitators, mesmerists, and radical utopians who wanted to get back to the land. ("Latin farmers," they were called, because all their knowledge of farming came out of Virgil's *Georgics*.)

There was only one thing all these people agreed on: Catholics weren't to be trusted. There were a lot of reasons. Catholics owed their primary loyalty neither to the old country nor the new, but to the sinister pope sunk in the corruptions of Rome; they held weird rituals involving blood; their confession box was a fount of indecency. One of the most popular forms of literature in those days was the hard-hitting mock-journalistic exposé of the secrets of the Catholic Church. These were widely distributed and avidly read—with good reason. Once you got past the somber introductory warnings, they proved to be about the adventures of lascivious priests and the goings-on in orgiastic nunneries.

So Catholics like the Sehnerts had to be discreet. Their parish church was a modest white clapboard steeple house hidden down a meandering dirt road. Most Sundays there was no priest. Catholic priests were rare sights in southern Illinois in those days; one could be counted on to pass through Greenville only a couple of times a year. That meant no mass, no confession, and no communion—only a devotional meeting conducted by the parishioners themselves, following guidelines supplied by the local church hierarchy. (Church officials assured the faithful that, whatever it might say in the catechism, private repentance was acceptable in the eyes of God if there was no priest available to hear confessions.) A Protestant spy would have been bitterly disappointed; the services were decorous and mouse-timid compared to the ecstatic, raftershaking revival meetings of their neighbors.

Things were just as restrained at the Sehnert farm. There were no images of the Virgin on display, no crucifixes, no catechisms. The family didn't own a Bible. The only mystical book that Peter was ever observed perusing was the *Farmers' Almanac*.

But this is not to say there was no spiritual drama in Peter Sehnert's life. The way the family remembers him, there was nothing in his life but spiritual drama. He was the archetype of the thundering patriarch, half hard-hearted farmer and half Old Testament prophet—the sort of man who saw the hand of God in everything, from early frosts to summer droughts, from the weakness of a newborn baby to the vigor of a young calf.

Men like Peter knew what God demanded of them: unceasing struggle against unforgiving odds. Peter's standards were passed down to his descendants. My family has always been contemptuous of the lazy, the weak, the self-pitying, the fallen, and the soft—the categories into which Peter assigned just about everyone he ever met. He regarded such people as being fit only to be cheated. So while nobody ever forgot his rages, even more memorable was the sight of his rare, deep-glowing bliss when he got the better of a neighbor in a business deal.

Otherwise, his chief glory was his solitude. He took no interest whatsoever in the outside world. He was not known to spread gossip or listen to rumors or read newspapers or pass the time of day with anyone. Whole days went by without his saying a word to his wife and children.

This wasn't an uncommon way of life. The heartland was scattered with immigrant families doing just what the Sehnerts did—not so much starting their lives over as starting the world over, like Noah and his family after the flood. Many were seen in town only twice a year, at spring planting and at harvest; they'd do their business as quickly and tersely as they could and then ride out again, vanishing down the ragged dirt tracks between cornfields to resume their existence alone with God.

There used to be a story in the family—it was still current in my childhood—about just how isolated Peter was. They said that he was wholly oblivious to the Civil War (or, as they called it in Illinois, the War of the Rebellion). He was too old to fight, and his sons too young, so the whole event passed him by. He finally learned about it one spring morning when he was out working in the fields. That was when he heard a mysterious noise: a sweet, distant humming that seemed to come floating toward him from all directions, fading and surging again as though it were emanating from the land itself. The church bells were ringing out to proclaim that the Union had been preserved.

Peter's idyll lasted more than twenty years. But history finally caught up with him after the war. Agricultural prices went into a catastrophic decline, and farms throughout the Midwest began failing. Peter was a stubborn man and kept going through several disastrous seasons. But at last his health and his finances were ruined. He lost the farm in the mid-1870s and he died soon afterward.

Peter's oldest son, John Louis, took over as head of the family. Nobody thought he was half the man his father was. He had no interest in farming, in hard work generally, or in a life of righteous isolation. Even in his early childhood he was running away from the farm; he'd escape into town and spend the day with the idle kids outside the general store, until his silently ferocious father arrived to collect him. Nor did he have any use for religion. In later life he had a taste for gambling and for the ladies; he would blandly lie about this to the priest each week and complacently kneel for communion.

But he did inherit one thing from Peter: a love of making deals. He liked to be known as a sharp businessman, in an age when "sharp" meant something close to "outright larcenous." When he was a young man, he started going by his initials, because "J. L. Sehnert" made him sound more like a tycoon.

Soon after his father died, J.L. met and married a town girl named Franciska Spengel. She was from a German Catholic family who lived in Highland, Illinois. She had no more desire to be a farmer's wife than J.L. did to be a farmer—so they borrowed money from her parents and opened a hotel in the small town of Pierron.

Pierron was a wholly typical Illinois farming community. It was a cluster of freshly built houses around a train station deep in the countryside. The houses were white clapboard, with peaked roofs and railed front porches, and their neatly manicured lawns were edged by flower beds and ringed by picket fences. The business district consisted of a barbershop, a feed barn, a general store, and a smithy. There was also a government building made of stone that served as a combination courthouse, county clerk's office, jail, and emergency storm shelter. The total population was around two hundred people, and rather more chickens, cows, horses, and pigs.

Pierron had never seen anything like J.L.'s hotel. It was a smart two-story building with a sprawling stable attached. Above the door was a big carved sign bearing the slogan *The Oakdale House—Ample Entertainment for Man and Beast*. Its saloon had brass railings and a bar of varnished wood; on the second story were rooms to let, spartan but clean, with fresh linen on the beds and lace curtains on the windows. The hotel caused a sensation when it opened. The saloon immediately became the unofficial town hall, and everybody knew to look there first for the sheriff, the justice of the peace, and the local notary.

J.L. and Franciska had several good years in Pierron. Their first children were born there in the winter of 1875, in the attic room above the Oakdale's saloon: twins George and Mary. George was a weak child, but he survived; Mary died in infancy—nobody bothered to record why. The third child was my great-grandfather John Sebastian, afterward known as Bosh. He was born in January 1876; the town barber (who doubled as the doctor) was in attendance, while J.L. tended bar downstairs. It was said in the family that Bosh arrived in the middle of a blizzard so fierce the bar's customers never noticed the cries of either the mother or the child.

In the mid-1880s, the citizens of Pierron finally got around to naming the streets so the post office could make regular deliveries. They strained their imaginations to come up with Main Street and Railroad Street. But there was no debate at all about what to call the dirt track in front of the Oakdale. It was named Sehnert Street. To this day, that's the biggest honor anybody in my family has received.

But the Oakdale never made much money. While the

saloon did a steady business, the rooms were almost always empty. J.L. had to come up with countless short-term schemes to keep the place afloat. His best idea was to buy newfangled farm equipment, train his hotel employees as operators, and lease them out to local farmers for the spring planting and the fall harvest. When this didn't make him rich, he gave up. He sold the hotel in the summer of 1888, and he and his family left Pierron for Edwardsville.

Edwardsville was the biggest town in the county. In fact, its population of three thousand made it one of the biggest towns in Illinois. To modern eyes, it would have looked like an idealized image of bucolic peace: it was a cluster of slanted roofs and white church steeples nestled among green forested hills. But its inhabitants thought of it as a bustling industrial zone. It had coal mines, machine shops, factories, and several towering flour mills. (These last were notorious fire hazards, and over the years they all went up in titanic blazes that the whole town gathered to watch.) It also had a big commercial district. The streets were unpaved, and in summer the reek of the horses was overpowering, but the storefronts were brick and stone, and several blocks had even been wired with electric streetlights. They were switched on from dusk to midnight whenever it was cloudy.

The town was also large enough to support an old-fashioned, fully articulated class system, of the notoriously suffocating heartland variety. There were aristocrats in hedge-hidden mansions, who measured out their lives by cotillions and charity balls; there was a relentlessly churchgoing middle class; and there was a rowdy working class, whose taste in entertainment ran to burlesque revues and raree-shows. There was also a thriving German community. As in a lot of downstate towns, the German-born and their children made up between a third and a half of the total population. The Germans had their own groceries and bakeries and meat markets; they had their own newspapers (brought in from Saint Louis and Chicago); there were classes conducted in German in the public schools; many of the Protestant churches had regular services in German, and the German Catholics had their own parish church, strictly segregated from the Irish—it was an imposing stone building that stood across from the town square, with its own full-time priest.

There were ten hotels and rooming houses in town. They too had a caste structure. The top of the line was fancy indeed: the Saint James Hotel. It was at the heart of the commercial district. It was three stories of pale, elegant brick topped by a mansard roof. The interior had plush carpeting, deep-varnished mahogany, and polished brass. It even had an eight-hundred-seat theater where local drama clubs and visiting professional companies staged performances—though it was called an opera house, not a theater, because "theater" was a vulgar word; it connoted burlesque.

J.L.'s new hotel was far down the scale from there. It was a two-story clapboard building, with a saloon on the ground floor and the rooms to rent upstairs. It stood on the southwest edge of town, in an area of recently cleared woodland along the new commuter railroad corridor, a couple of hundred yards down from the station. "Sehnert's Hotel" was painted in huge letters just beneath the roofline to catch the eye of new arrivals peering around uncertainly on the platform.

Sehnert's Hotel was austere. The beds were hard; the saloon was dark and loud. But it was a popular and prosperous business from the first. (German-run saloons and hotels were preferred by the Anglo working and middle classes, because they had a reputation for cleanliness and propriety.) The clientele were commercial travelers, itinerant craftsmen, laborers looking for work at the local factories, and farmers up from the country for a day or two to buy equipment and supplies— anybody, in short, who'd be impressed by its slogan: *First-class Service, Reasonable Rates, Courteous Treatment.*

In the saloon, the regulars were local workmen and clerks and small businessmen, anyone who wanted to sit around and drink Sehnert's beers and ales (brewed in the hotel basement) and get into furious arguments about the burning issues of the day: Free Silver, Farmers' Alliances, signs of the End Times. Sometimes a traveler brought out a fiddle and played for drinks—an old country air, or a mournful ballad about the assassination of President Garfield. There was a battered upright in back where a regular would pound out tunes. When the men danced, the unvarnished plank flooring thumped and rumbled like a drum.

I have a family heirloom that suggests something about the quality of their lives. It's an authentic Sehnert's Hotel coffee cup. Doubtless the Saint James served its coffee in enameled china with floral patterns; at Sehnert's it came in a featureless, unglazed, off-white mug as thick as an elephant's hide. The absence of a handle was part of its practical design. It was intended to be filled with scaldingly hot coffee and clasped firmly between both palms. That was the only warmth a workingman was likely to feel in his hands in the course of a long winter's day.

The hotel was a great success for J.L. But he never attained the social status in Edwardsville that he'd known in Pierron. His name pops up here and there in the town records and in period newspapers, usually among the donors to charitable causes—but never at the glittering top of the list, only in the gray, prudent lower middle. He was a member of the German-American businessmen's lodge, the Druids—a respectable lodge, but not socially of the first rank. The prestigious Anglo lodges, the Freemasons and Odd Fellows, never invited him to join. And, of course, nobody ever offered to name a street after him. In Edwardsville a saloon wasn't a fit business for the best people.

He grew to be the model of the classic barkeep. He had a moon face, a hatchet nose, and a shock of salt-and-pepper hair. He was powerfully muscled but carried a big gut behind his barman's apron. His manner was brusque and his English guttural. He was famous for his needling, malicious sense of humor. "A great kidder," people called him—which didn't mean he was funny, exactly; it meant that he really knew how to get under your skin.

People also said he was a great ladies' man. He flirted, ponderously and relentlessly, with every woman he met, from the neighborhood matrons to the chambermaids. Franciska looked the other way—it was what she expected of any man.

But he had another flaw neither she nor anybody else in the family could forgive: he was lazy. For all J.L.'s scheming, Franciska did the real work of running the hotel.

Nobody ever called Franciska lazy. She was one of those iron-willed Victorian matrons who saw life as backbreaking labor with no hope of earthly reward. In family photographs she invariably appears in a forbiddingly heavy, out-of-season ankle-length dress, and her face is frozen in a mask of stony suspicion and disapproval. If she took any joy at all in existence— and I've never heard anybody claim she did—she found it in the flourishing of her family and the steadiness of her faith.

Her marriage to J.L. may not have been happy, but she never thought happiness was the point. Obedience was—if not to him, then to her church and her culture. She attended mass three times a week, and she was highly disapproving of the priest for his lackluster penances. She had no use whatever for the life outside. She never traveled as far away from home as Saint Louis, she spoke nothing but German with her family and friends, and she learned only as much English as she absolutely had to, to deal with customers and tradespeople at the hotel. She took "be fruitful and multiply" to be the fundamental commandment. She had seven children, six of whom survived infancy, and they all grew up with her stern presence at the center of their world.

She set the children to work at the hotel almost as soon as they were old enough to walk. They made the beds and emptied the chamber pots; they scoured out the cuspidors and swept the vomit-clotted sawdust from the saloon floor. The candles and the oil lamps deposited a thick layer of greasy soot on every surface, so the walls and floors had to be scrubbed every few days, and the upholstery and curtains had to be washed weekly. And there was a ceaseless avalanche of laundry. The linens and the bedsheets were spectacularly foul, since they were used by guests who rarely bathed more than once a month.

Before school each day the children waited and bused tables in the dining room. That was their biggest job. Hotels like Sehnert's were expected to lay out a staggering breakfast— every morning there'd be fried steak, eggs, pancakes, honey-cured ham, pork sausages, fresh biscuits in bacon gravy, and fruit pie. Lunch and dinner were lighter: usually cold meats, hard-boiled eggs, fresh-baked bread, and boiled potatoes; they were set out on a buffet table at the back of the saloon.

The customers were demanding and brusque, and tipping was unknown. Instead the children were routinely cuffed or slapped by customers for making mistakes.

At the end of the day, the children slept in a stifling cubby-hole at the back of the attic, with two narrow beds and a window overlooking the train tracks. Even then the work wasn't done. When trains arrived after sunset, one of the boys would be roused by the night clerk, and he'd have to go over to the station and greet the passengers piling down onto the dark platform. Winter or summer, with snow piled high along the tracks or cicadas shrieking in the weeds, the boy would wait till the noise of the train died down, and then he'd hold up a lantern and cry, "Hotel, hotel, hotel!"

The children all went to an English-speaking public school. Unlike their mother, they were eager to assimilate. They worked hard at speaking accent-free English—that is, whenever Franciska was out of earshot. They also shed their German names just as soon as they hit the school yard. The oldest son, George Adolph, developed a lifelong amnesia about his middle name. The youngest sons, Wilhelm Louis and Emil Richard, were always called Louie and Dick. The youngest daughter, Hermina, became Minnie. The oldest, Franciska, named for her mother, first called herself Frances and then settled on Daisy.

None of them made it past the eighth grade. There was

no need for more learning when the course of their lives was so clear—the boys would go into their father's business, and the girls would get married, have children, and work as hard as or harder than Franciska did. Their education had been made up mostly of memorizing rules—rules of English grammar, arithmetic, and long, cumbersome systems of weights and measures, rods and poods and yards and bushels and dry quarts. But there had been other lessons as well, and these the children wholly absorbed. They became unquestioning believers in all the books' homilies about duty and practicality and cheerful obedience, which were illustrated by stern warnings about children who defied their parents and were immediately trampled to death by speeding milk wagons. To the end of their lives, they lived as though the schoolbook version of morality were the only kind possible. Or most of them did, anyway.

2

Bosh's Only Idea

JOHN SEBASTIAN SEHNERT, my great-grandfather, was an odd man. From his earliest childhood, people shook their heads over him and said he was bound to come to no good. He was an idler, a woolgatherer, indifferent to authority, dreamily impervious to punishment, unintimidated by anybody else's opinions. At school, he perversely insisted on re-Germanizing his name, by pronouncing it in the heaviest Teutonic accent he could muster: yo-hann say-BOSH-tyan. When the other kids made fun of him he just laughed and repeated their jokes himself. That was how his friends and even his family came to call him Bosh.

The name stuck; it suited him. He had a lifelong love of bosh, of nonsense and irrelevant fantasy. He loved bad jokes and worse puns; he invented childish parodies of popular songs and sang them with operatic passion. He was the class clown, the goof, the one who couldn't stop laughing at the silly names in the schoolbooks. To the end of his days he thought education meant high-sounding nonsense made up of equal parts Cicero and Hiawatha.

His only real talent was for playing hooky. He practiced it incessantly—sometimes his brothers had to escort him forcibly into the schoolhouse to keep him from flunking out. His real education was in geography. He learned every road and creek and woodland for miles around Edwardsville. He knew every barn and backcountry church, every derelict cabin, every farmhouse where he could cadge a free lunch, every fenced-in shack where a family kept its lunatic relative—the wild-eyed uncle who'd nailed up hex signs to ward off the evil eye and would wildly charge at trespassers from the cornrows while shouting verses from Revelation.

Bosh did manage to finish the eighth grade. After that he had a meandering career around town. There was always a relative or a family friend or a business associate of his father's who'd help him out with a menial job. Over his teenage years he was a grocery clerk, a telegraph messenger, a photographer's assistant, and a shoe salesman. His employers were always taken by his air of kindheartedness and imperturbability, and always ended up exasperated to a fury by his daydreaming.

His longest-lasting job was as a train conductor. When he was nineteen he got hired by a midsize passenger line that ran between Toledo and Topeka. He worked the milk run from Saint Louis to Springfield. It lasted for a couple of years. But he never liked it much. In those days train travel in the Midwest was famous for swarming confusion. Every car was a carnival of salesmen, remittance men, immigrant families, preachers, hustlers, and drifters. He was worn out by the sight of them and made homesick by the interminable vistas of unfamiliar farmland streaming past the tracks. Eventually he quit and resumed his aimless life around town.

He became a familiar sight in Edwardsville's saloons. People said he was the only one of the Sehnert boys who'd rather be a saloon's customer than its owner. He became a fiend for billiards, which he mastered in endless afternoons of solitary practice. He got to the point where he could beat just about anybody in town. He started playing for money and picked up enough to indulge a newfound taste for fine clothes. He learned to wear suits fashionably loose, the tie and handkerchief just slightly askew. In this attire he strolled into the classiest billiard rooms downtown, the ones with green baize and polished brass and varnished mahogany; he carried himself with the negligent grace of a riverboat gambler come ashore for a day's amusement. Even as he trounced his opponents, he treated them with grave respect—so grave, in fact, that nobody could tell whether he was kidding.

His father put an end to this career. J.L. understood laziness all too well, but he wasn't going to watch any son of his make a fool of himself. So he took Bosh into the family business and gave him the one job everybody thought he could handle: deliveryman.

So twice a week Bosh loaded up a big beer wagon and drove its horses between Edwardsville and Pierron and Highland. He liked the job—particularly the solitude. Usually he rode alone, with a shotgun in case of hijackers, and he had nothing to do except watch the familiar hills and forests drift past. Still, it wasn't as easy as it sounds. The roads hadn't changed much since the days of the first settlers. They were fine in the summer, when they were baked solid by the sun and softened by dust, and they were passable in winter, after the ruts had been filled in with ice and hard-packed snow. But the thaws of spring and the long rains of fall made them a soupy misery: a journey of a few hours could turn into a day and night of torture as the wagon lurched from one bottomless mud hole to the next. Bosh took pride in his growing skill at maneuvering through the maze.

But it was the sight of him perched atop the wagon that finished him off in the eyes of the town. A hundred years later, one of the local gossips could still remember the judgment passed on him then. "Everybody liked Bosh," she told me. "But they all said the same thing about him. His problem was, he just had no ambition."

Sehnert's Hotel was notorious for the speed at which it ran through hired help. Those were hard times, the 1890s, the worst that America would see until the Great Depression; a lot of people were out of work, on the road, grateful for any day labor they could scrabble up. But even so, some of the hardiest cooks and maids and clerks couldn't endure the ferocity of Franciska's taskmastering—and of the women who could, most were scared off by J.L.'s lumbering, undeflectable flirtatiousness. It wasn't until the turn of the century that they found a chambermaid who proved resistant to both.

Her name was Agnes Gross. She was twenty-one. She was broad and big-boned, with a flat nose, a wide, plain face, and masses of dull brown hair. She had a spectacular temper. No one was better at conveying furious resentment at Franciska's demands, and her look of sullen hatred whenever J.L. contrived to be alone with her was enough to get even an elephant like him to shy off. But she had one other quality that trumped any of her defects in the Sehnerts' eyes. She had a limitless capacity for hard work.

Agnes had been born in the town of Alhambra, about fifteen miles east of Edwardsville. Her family was much like the Sehnerts; in fact, they'd come from the same Rhinelander province and had similar success in America as farmers and tradespeople. Agnes's brothers were pharmacists and grocers; a couple had been gandy dancers on the railroad; one opened the county's first telephone service—he had forty clients, and his wife operated the switchboard from a curtained alcove in their parlor. And, like the Sehnerts, the family had a faint hint of the disreputable hovering over them, though in their case it dated from a single incident. Agnes's father, August, had been a wagon maker until his factory burned down in the mid-1870s. Decades later, people in Alhambra were still saying darkly that the fire had been no accident.

Agnes had been on her own since she was fourteen. She'd never gotten along with her family; she was iron-willed and disobedient and she'd run away several times while still in grammar school. Once she'd left home for good, she spent years working in factories and living in cheap rooming houses. In her late teens she came to Edwardsville and drifted into domestic service. Sehnert's was the first hotel she'd worked at, and she hadn't decided yet whether it would be her last. She didn't have much use for her employers and was thinking of moving on—that is, until she met Bosh.

He was twenty-four then: a good-humored young man with a round face, disorderly hair, and kindly eyes. He was known to everyone as a ne'er-do-well and a soft touch, someone who couldn't be trusted to carry out the simplest errand, but who would empty his pockets to the last penny if a friend or a new acquaintance or a passerby were in need. When he began to notice Agnes—hanging around the hotel in the afternoons as she made the beds, fearlessly teasing her when she was in a foul mood—she couldn't tell whether he was imitating his father (with far more delicacy) or taking pity on a plain girl. It was a long time before she would admit to herself that he was serious.

His family had no idea what to make of this romance. On the whole, they approved—J.L. was heard to say that Agnes was just the girl who could beat some sense into Bosh.

But there was a sticking point, at least for Franciska: Agnes was a devout Lutheran. The crisis was resolved when she agreed to convert to Catholicism. It was the only instance on record where she did anything for the sake of somebody else's feelings.

Bosh and Agnes were married in March 1902. The custom of a church wedding with the bride in white wasn't common then among German Catholics; the service was at the priest's house, and Agnes proudly wore a new blue dress. The wedding day was brilliant—cloudless, windy, and warm, the first thaw of spring. The streets of Edwardsville became rivers of mud, and Bosh's skill as a driver failed him—a few blocks from home the bridal carriage got stuck up to its axles. His efforts to free it grew so ornately frantic that the whole wedding party was caught up in a wave of giddy hilarity, and everyone arrived at the priest's house disheveled, mud-spattered, and teary-eyed with laughter.

The newlyweds moved into their own room at the back of the hotel's second floor. There was inevitably some gossip around town about the speed of their engagement and why a hotel owner's son would marry a chambermaid. But it was silenced when the first child, my grandfather Clarence, was born a decorous eleven months after the wedding.

Bosh's older brother George was an artist—everybody said so. When he was a teenager he was apprenticed to a local brewmaster, and afterward he started brewing beers and ales for Sehnert's Hotel. He concocted the sweetest pilsners, the most chocolaty bocks, the fizziest weisses, and the richest spiced Christmas ales. Sehnert's became one of the most popular brands in town, and orders poured in from saloons and taverns all over the county. J.L. had to expand the brewery; he moved it out of the hotel basement and rented space at a warehouse downtown. When the money started flowing in, he decided to sell the hotel and run the brewery full-time.

It was a seller's market. After the Spanish-American War, the new century had brought boom times to the heartland. J.L. waited for the right buyer, closed a deal shortly after New Year's 1905, and immediately bought a big new house for the family.

The house was on Brown Street, a quiet residential street on the southeast side of town. It was a squat, solid brownstone—the sort of solemnly respectable place where the blinds were kept drawn and the afternoon stillness was deepened by the tock of the grandfather clock. But J.L. liked things lively. He filled the house with family and friends: three generations of Sehnerts and a floating population of visitors, houseguests, and out-of-town cousins. It was a rare meal when fifteen or twenty people didn't sit down together at the dining room table.

Meanwhile the new owner of the hotel bought almost everything in it: the bedsteads, the unmonogrammed sheets, the anonymous mugs and plates and coffee cups. All he needed to do was paint out "Sehnert's Hotel" on the clapboard and paint in "Liebler's Hotel." There was only one item he had no use for: a newly arrived box of Sehnert's Hotel letterhead. That J.L. brought home with him.

I have one of those pages in front of me now. Somebody has used it to write a brief account in German of J.L.'s life— the childhood on the farm, the Oakdale House in Pierron, the move to Edwardsville. Scrawled across the top in English is: *Died 12:40 AM 25th day of December 1905.*

J.L. was fifty-five and strong as an ox. But in those days death came with little or no warning, from any of a thousand untrace- able causes; that was a time when even an unnoticed blister could prove fatal. Part of the gossip that circulated daily across the back fences and along the laundry lines all over town was who had fallen mysteriously ill, who had died overnight, who had been seen only yesterday looking in the pink of health. All that the Sehnert children and grandchildren ever knew about J.L.'s death was this: from then on, Christmas at the Brown Street house was a day of mourning.

The oldest son, George, took over as head of the family and proprietor of the business. It didn't take long for everybody to realize he wasn't cut out for either job. He was a niggler and a worrier, quick to fire anybody who challenged him and maniacally suspicious about being cheated. At home he proved an overbearing tyrant who presided gloomily over the dinner table and lashed out at anybody who dared to lighten the mood.

It wasn't long before he started losing both workers and dinner guests. Bosh, the least valuable employee, was the first out the door.

Bosh had grown somber and preoccupied since his father's death. For the first time in his life he'd started to talk about moving out and buying a place of his own. After he quit the brewery, he took a job of uncharacteristic seriousness: apprentice machinist with a local freight railroad company. He worked at the roundhouse—a loud, smoky, sweltering place filled with the shriek and clang of metal on metal and the roar of escaping steam. The work was exhausting and dangerous, but Bosh was at last learning the rudiments of a trade. He impressed everybody by displaying a previously unsuspected capacity for backbreaking work.

Each day he walked to and from the roundhouse along Troy Road, the main highway south out of town. A few blocks from Brown Street it led him past the last house and into the countryside. It was no longer the untouched world out there that it had been in his childhood; there were now several big blotches of new construction. He passed a brick factory with a churning smokestack, a brass foundry, and a huddle of makeshift wooden buildings around the shaft of a coal mine. Bosh had to walk an extra half mile or so before the pristine stillness of the prairie resumed. There, in the summertime, the rustling of the tall grass and the buzzing of bees could still be heard hundreds of yards away, and in the winter the snow hissed like snakes along distant lines of fence posts. There was rarely any traffic. The clop of a horse resounded minutes ahead of its arrival, and the rumble of a wagon gathered strength as slowly as a thunderstorm.

Another half mile down the road was a rail crossing. Bosh followed the tracks west to a cluster of spurs and sidings, where the roundhouse and the repair barns stood. The land on either side of the tracks was sparse and meandering, poor soil for farming. That was why Bosh was so surprised to see on his commute, one spring morning in 1907, men alongside the tracks with surveying gear.

He knew at once what it meant. Somebody was interested in buying up the land and building houses. He then had the only big practical idea of his life. If he acted quickly, he could still afford to buy land there and build a house himself.

He'd never even considered being a property owner before and had no idea how to go about it. His brothers had to arrange everything for him. But that wasn't too difficult; the boom times in Edwardsville meant that banks were eager to lend. All Bosh really needed to get a mortgage was a couple of hundred dollars up front and proof of a steady job. His brothers decided that the money was his fair share of their father's estate; and as for the job, they encouraged him to apply at the N. O. Nelson Manufacturing Company, the prestige employer of blue-collar workers in Edwardsville.

The Nelson company manufactured fine porcelain and brass plumbing fixtures. It was the creation of an eccentric industrialist, one of the last of the nineteenth-century experimenters in utopian philosophy. His factories—a brass foundry and a porcelain shop—were models of modern design: long, low buildings with rows of immense arched windows and double rows of skylights, ivy flourishing on the walls of whitewashed brick. They stood in the grassy fields to the east of Troy Road, looking like newfangled greenhouses.

Nelson also built housing for his workers where he could put his ideas and whims into practice. He carved a whole new village out of the woodlands southeast of town. He named it Leclaire. Leclaire had generously sized houses on elegantly curving streets; the streets were named after Nelson's heroes: Longfellow, Lincoln, Ruskin. There were no local laws or police officers, and an elaborate barter system was used in place of money at the village stores. Even Bosh, who wasn't about to give up his new property to live in Leclaire, still shared in employee benefits unheard-of at ordinary factories, such as free medical and dental care.

But once Bosh started at his job, he discovered that the aura of modernity stopped at the foundry door. The fury of the cauldron, the endless roils of steam and smoke, the dancing shadows of the work crews, the squeals and hisses of the molten brass, the shriek of the drills, and the peacock-tail plumes of sparks from the saws—it was all overwhelming and intoxicating on first exposure. But there was little about it that would have baffled a brass worker from the Renaissance.

Bosh quickly got the hang of it. Nelson didn't believe in specialization; every employee was expected to understand the operation of the whole plant. So Bosh learned his trade in a steady circuit down the hall and back again. He began at the cauldron. This was where a crew used long, charred oars to stir a fierce sludge of copper and zinc. They periodically dumped in a load of hissing salt (to flux the oxides) and the scraps and defective castings left over from the last shift. In the middle of the hall were other teams of workmen. They were setting the enormous mazelike sand molds. To save time, the foundry made dozens of pieces in a single cast, so after the bellowing alarm, when the cauldron was tilted and the molten sludge was poured, after the cast had cooled and the fused sand was scoured away, what was revealed was a surreal tree of pipes hung with dangling faucet-fruit. At the far end of the hall was another team with saws and drills; they cut the tree apart and loaded the pieces into hoppers, which they rolled out the main doors toward the shipping department on the other side of the grassy plaza.

After Bosh completed his first successful circuit through the foundry he was instructed to repeat it; after that to repeat it again. Then he was promoted to shop foreman. It was the most responsible position he'd ever achieved, and it proved to be the furthest reach of his ambitions. He stayed at the job for the rest of his life.

In less than a year Bosh owned three adjoining plots along the railroad tracks—almost a third of an acre of land—and his house was ready for occupancy. It was a spartan place even by the austere standards of the day. There were four rooms: kitchen, dining room, bedroom, and parlor (which, as was the custom, was strictly reserved for guests), plus a basement pantry and an attic. It had a coal furnace but no electricity or plumbing. Freshwater was drawn from a hand pump in the yard by the kitchen door, and there was a two-seater outhouse by the back fence.

He and Agnes furnished the house at a bankruptcy auction for a nearby farm; they came home with a load of carved chairs and knobby bedsteads and a battered but magnificent oak table for the dining room. The walls in the kitchen were whitewashed; in the rest of the house, they put up fashionably dark floral wallpaper. They hung three pieces of art in the parlor: a tinted lithograph of Abraham Lincoln, a second of Lincoln giving the Gettysburg Address, and a third of Lincoln on his deathbed titled *Now He Belongs to the Ages*. Out back, in the huge yard, Bosh planted a vegetable garden and a little orchard of peach trees.

The family and Bosh's friends all thought a little house along the railroad was a step down from the house on Brown

Street. But that didn't matter to Bosh; he loved the place the moment he first set foot in it. Many years later, toward the end of his life, he told his daughter Helen that every time he returned to his house, even from a trip to the grocery store, the sight of it made his heart leap.

3

The Last of the Old Country

IN 1910 A commercial traveler for a big Midwestern brewery passed through Edwardsville and happened to sample
Sehnert's Ale. He was so impressed that he immediately sought
out George Sehnert and offered him a job as a brewmaster.
The brewery was in Joliet, on the other side of the state—but
George accepted on the spot. A month later, he and his wife
and children left Edwardsville and never came back.

That was the end of the family business. Nobody even
considered hiring another brewmaster; they knew they'd
never find one as good as George. They sold off the brewery
and left the last remaining kegs of George's finest to go cloudy
and sour at the back of the warehouse. It wasn't long before
George's art was forgotten. Only the family remembered the
stories of how good the beer had been—but not so much as

an empty bottle or a label has survived among the family's heirlooms.

George's departure was also the signal for a more general exodus from the Brown Street house. The next to go were his brothers Louie and Dick; they opened a small saloon in the old German neighborhood on the north side of town, and when that proved to be a success, they each bought a house nearby. (After Prohibition came in and the saloon was closed down, Louie took up farming; Dick, who had a head for figures, became a land surveyor for the county.) Their sister Daisy married a man named Joseph Maclean who worked with Bosh at the Nelson company; they moved into a little house in Leclaire. The last daughter, Minnie, married a grocer named Jim Revelle. She soon accompanied him back to Topeka, Kansas, where he'd inherited the family business.

That left old Franciska. In 1905, she and J.L. had moved into the house to preside over a brood of children and grand-children; ten years later she was living in the house alone.

Franciska didn't take well to solitude. She grew querulous and demanding, much given to bending the ears of visitors about her unworthy children. Her particular target was Bosh. Bosh was the only one of the children to come by regularly and to stay longer than duty required. She never tired of calling him a fool to his face, while praising him to everybody else as her lone example of filial piety. He never got angry with her. He insisted on bringing along his children and filling the

Brown Street house with their giddy, door-slamming, silence-shattering vitality. He even managed to coax Franciska out of the house for the occasional carriage ride around town.

Franciska hated most of what she saw. In those years the town was making a grand gesture of welcome to the new century by paving the streets. The commercial district had already been torn up; concrete sidewalks had replaced the wooden planking, and rows of electric streetlights were sprouting like vines. Now the work crews were invading the residential neighborhoods. The soft clop of hooves on dust was replaced by the rattle of wheels on brick; the new streetlights lit the town up all night, and over every main street and intersection, trolley wires dangled.

A bigger calamity awaited her. When the Great War came, her immediate family was spared; her sons were too old to serve and her grandsons too young. But the German culture of Edwardsville disappeared overnight. German stores changed their names and pulled their German-made goods from the shelves (or risked having their windows broken); schools dropped their German classes and churches their German services; anybody heard speaking German on the streets was taunted and sometimes physically harassed—it wasn't unusual for children to throw rocks at German speakers while their parents cheered them on.

Nor did any of the old culture reemerge from hiding after the war was over. On those rare times when Franciska left the house she found few traces of the world she remembered. Everybody spoke English on the streets and in the stores; most of her grandchildren didn't know a word of German. Only a scattering of old street signs—Krafft Street, Schwarz Street, Eberhardt Avenue—remained to prove that Germans had ever been in Edwardsville.

There were bonfires at the crossroads on Halloween, and fireworks in the parks on Decoration Day; the churches were standing room only on Easter and Christmas, and all church bells rang out at the stroke of midnight on New Year's Eve. People went to Wild West shows in the town square and saw theatrical companies put on shows at the opera house. On any clear, warm evening, Bosh and Agnes could walk with their children across Troy Road to Leclaire Lake, where people swam and strolled on the grass as a brass band played. The calendar was crowded with fish fries and church dances and ice-cream socials; every week there was at least one occasion when the whole town gathered.

During the dog days of summer, the Chautauqua came through. Full-page ads and schedules of events were published in the local paper, and the clerks in stores all over town sported big red-white-and-blue buttons that read *I'm Going!* and *I've Got My Ticket!* The Chautauqua was held in a wide meadow in the open country east of town. Every day for a week, people swarmed out to its tents to hear oompah concerts, lurid arias from operettas, solemnly edifying lectures, and sword-clacking enactments of scenes from classic drama. It was a sort of tamed and secularized relic of the wild revival meetings and river baptisms of the old times.

And there were parades—for national holidays and local ones, for any reason or none at all. The town was always eager to spend an afternoon cheering. Sometimes it seemed as though history manifested itself only in the changing procession of floats. At the centennial parade of 1914, the automobile made its first major incursion. Cars were still rare sights then, and it would be decades before horse-drawn wagons altogether disappeared from downtown. But the cars came down the parade route in a chugging, rattling, exhaust-banging line, draped in bunting and swarmed by brilliant balloons, every auto in private hands in the county. There were fifty of them in all.

At Bosh's house on Second Avenue, it sometimes seemed as if history would never arrive. "Second Avenue" had a grand sound, but it was still only a ragged dirt track off Troy Road. The nearest streetlight was a mile away, and from the front porch on any clear night you could see the Milky Way in full flood above the trees. There were times in winter, as the house shook in a blizzard, when it seemed as lonely and isolated as a pioneer homestead. When they were snowed in, Bosh would gather the family around the kitchen stove and tell stories—

the terrifying folktales he'd heard in his own childhood about the witches' sabbaths in the forest glades and the Erlking riding in mad pursuit down winter roads at night, hungry for children's souls. At other times he would give dramatic readings of the Sunday funnies: as the wind roared in the chimney and snow pelted the windows he would act out the latest antics of the Katzenjammer Kids or hold his audience spellbound with Little Nemo's voyage to Mars.

Bosh and Agnes had six children. The oldest, my grandfather Clarence, seemed to everyone like a throwback to the early days of the family. He had the old Sehnert look: stocky, firm, with a moon face and sharp nose and a bristling crop of wiry dark hair. He was a slow-talking, slow-thinking boy who had none of Bosh's easy camaraderie with strangers. But he did have a sense of humor—a peculiarly subterranean one that emerged only at the worst possible moments, in the form of jokes that he alone thought were funny. When he was a senior in high school, he was assigned Edwardsville's industry as a theme; he got up before the class, announced that he had chosen as his specific subject the local coal mines, and began, "Coal is black as hell."

That was as far as he got. The teacher sent him to the principal, and the principal expelled him. It was the standard penalty in those days for using profanity in school.

But Clarence was stubborn. He spent the following year idling around town; he took up pool and became almost as good as his father (his friends started calling him "Jasper," after a riverboat gambler in an old melodrama). But all the while he was determined to go back to school. The following fall he reapplied, repeated the twelfth grade—stone-faced and impervious to the teasing of his classmates—and graduated. He was the first of the Sehnerts to get a high school diploma. And he was the last, for another twenty years.

The second son, Oliver, died when he was a year and a half old. A note in the family records reads: *Scalded in the bath.* Maybe it was a sign the world was changing that somebody bothered to note a cause.

The oldest daughter, Pearl, was born two years after Oliver. She was strong, pretty, and exuberant. The town gossips said she was a good girl but maybe a little too eager to get out of the gate.

She dropped out of school when she was fifteen, and Bosh got her a job in the Nelson company shipping department. This was considered relatively dainty work—most of the crew were women. Pearl spent her day filling up crates with brass plumbing fixtures and porcelain sinks and toilet bowls; before she got used to it, her hands were chafed raw by the wood and the needlelike straw packing. The crates went from her station down the line to be nailed shut; then they were loaded up on skids and swung on a big winch out through the wide doors of the department to a boxcar waiting on a siding. Men worked the winch, and in the swelter of summer they shrugged aside their modesty with their shirts. One of the men was huge and loud, with a booming laugh and an odd, unplaceable accent. His name was Cecil Bilyeu.

People said Cecil had come up the Mississippi from Cajun country—an idea that lingers in the Sehnert family to this day. But the Bilyeus were in fact descendants of French trappers and homesteaders who'd settled Illinois hundreds of years before the first German or Englishman arrived. But wherever he might have come from, he stood out. Unlike the dour and proper inhabitants of Edwardsville, he was wild, profane, and openhearted, with a boundless appetite for good times. Almost as soon as he and Pearl started flirting with each other, they were having tumultuous fights and passionate reconciliations that were the talk of the Nelson company.

Bosh and Agnes didn't know how to deal with this crisis. Agnes was furious at Pearl and wanted to forbid her from seeing Cecil. Bosh came up with a compromise: Cecil could attend Sunday dinners at the Sehnerts' so long as he would promise never to see Pearl alone. Cecil agreed.

It wasn't an arrangement destined to last. A couple of

months later, Pearl turned sixteen. On Christmas Eve, she and Cecil worked a half shift at the Nelson company. They left the factory together. About what happened next, Cecil always liked to say, "We just couldn't think of anything better to do." They got in his battered truck and drove down the snow-buried roads to Greenville, Illinois, where they found a justice of the peace and got married.

They were too afraid of Agnes to tell her what they'd done. For weeks afterward they lived separately. Pearl went home to Second Avenue each night, while Cecil returned to the small house on the east side of town he shared with his mother and sister. It was Cecil's sister who put an end to the charade. One February day when Cecil was at work, she found the marriage license in his bedroom, and out of spite, she sent it to the local newspaper. The following morning Bosh was greeted at the foundry by friends congratulating him on his daughter's wedding.

Bosh got angry then. Everybody said they'd never seen him so angry. He marched out of the foundry and across to the shipping room, where he confronted Pearl and demanded an explanation. She confessed on the spot. He ordered her go home and tell her mother.

She left the shipping room in the middle of the shift and trudged home along Troy Road through the snow and fog. Afterward she thought of that as the most important walk of her life. She reached home and confessed to her mother. Agnes was furious—but Pearl refused to back down. She demanded to know what Agnes had against Cecil. Agnes drew herself up into a haughty silence, and then deflated.

"Oh, I like Cecil just fine," she said. "But it's never going to last. All you two ever do is fight."

And that was the end of the showdown. By the time Bosh returned from work, mother and daughter were reconciled. The next day Cecil took his bride home with him at the end of the shift, and for the first time they spent a whole night together.

Bosh and Agnes's second daughter, Hilda, was a different kind of rebel. She wore lots of makeup and bought glossy magazines to ogle the ads. In high school she hung around with a fast crowd. Most of Edwardsville's young people gathered at the roller rink after school, but Hilda sneaked out of the house at night and drove off with her friends to country roadhouses, where they drank bootleg beer and listened to jazz bands.

When she was sixteen, she told Bosh and Agnes she was going to drop out of school and become a saxophonist. Bosh shrewdly promised her that if she'd stay in school, he'd buy her a saxophone. She agreed, and Bosh presented her with a top-of-the-line model. She spent a few dismal weeks tormenting the house with bizarre blats and wails and groans. Then she announced that she wanted to drop out of school to become a secretary. This time Bosh promised her that if she'd stay in school, he'd buy her a typewriter. She practiced typing for one day; then the typewriter moved up to the attic to keep company with the sax.

The next time Hilda said she wanted to drop out, Bosh came up with a new deal: Hilda could quit school only if she'd agree to take care of old Franciska, who was still living alone in the Brown Street house and growing increasingly frail. Hilda accepted at once.

She had no idea what she was in for. Franciska was nearly blind, but she still wanted the house kept immaculately clean and orderly. She taught Hilda the ancient routine of households in Edwardsville, in which every day of the week had its specific dawn-to-dusk task. Monday was washing day, Tuesday ironing day, Wednesday housecleaning day, Thursday bread-baking day, Friday the day for shopping and soap making and sewing, Saturday for bathing and cake baking, Sunday for church and the family dinner at Bosh's house. (That was the only day when Franciska was willing to leave Brown Street.) The schedule was so strict that the sight of washing put out on the clothesline late in the week would bring all the neighbors over to find out what was wrong.

While drilling Hilda in clothes boiling and floor scrubbing and wallpaper scouring, and teaching her to always stir the soap clockwise as it was simmering (it was bad luck to stir the other way), Franciska bombarded her with an unending lecture on values. In the decades since J.L. had died, Franciska had hardened in her view of the world. It was imperative to be married. It was irrelevant whether one's husband was faithful. One owed one's husband utter obedience even if one despised him—because one's true obedience was to God, and a bad husband like J.L. was only a test that God had sent.

Listening to Franciska made Hilda bone-weary and heart-sick. But she stayed, and she learned.

The next son, Eugene, was a shy boy who sat silently at the dinner table with his head down and excused himself the instant his plate was clean. He never spoke in class, was an indifferent student, and barely managed to drag himself through to the tenth grade. Bosh got him a job at Nelson, and he spent a year learning how to cut and polish porcelain slabs into sinks and toilet bowls. He worked hard without ever losing his perpetual air of sullen distraction. All he really wanted was to be left alone, and his only genuine enthusiasm in life was hunting.

The countryside around Edwardsville was mostly fenced in and cultivated by then, and the big game of the old times was long gone. But farther from town there were woodlands and meadows where deer lingered, and marshlands swarming with waterfowl. Eugene took to spending days at a time out in the deep country. He was particularly fond of the area around Alhambra, the town where his mother had been born and where her family still lived.

In recent years there had been the beginnings of a cautious rapprochement between Agnes and her relatives—they said they'd be willing to talk to her again if she'd make some sort of conciliatory gesture, such as leave the Catholic Church, and she was considering doing it. When Eugene introduced himself, he was welcomed with open arms. He grew close to Agnes's brother August, who owned a big farm just outside of town. August gave Eugene permission to hunt in his fields and pastures, and often Eugene returned home to Edwardsville with rabbits, a deer haunch, and a couple of big buckets overflowing with wild blackberries and morel mushrooms.

On the farm Eugene made his best friend. This was August's younger brother, Frank. Frank was a reclusive figure who rarely left the farmhouse and didn't like to be approached too closely; he'd avoid eye contact and duck away as though looking for the nearest shadow. It was a legacy of his childhood, when he'd suffered such a bad case of eczema he couldn't go out in public. His family had homeschooled him and kept him soothed in ointments and swathed in loose wrappings of cotton, the only clothing he could tolerate. Nor had that been the end of his misfortunes. One day when he was ten, his brothers were shooting arrows at a fence and thought it would be funny to push him up behind the knothole they were using as a target; he lost an eye. He was somebody who, as the family said, "had a tough break in life."

But by the time Eugene met him, things had changed. He had been cured of his eczema—though nobody could say exactly how. The story came down in the family that "Frank met a doctor who suggested he try and rid himself of it, which he did." In any case Frank had grown up to be a gaunt but oddly handsome man with a roguish eye patch. He remained profoundly grateful to his brother August for taking him in. One of his nieces remembers: "Frank did everything for August. He kept house, cooked, canned, baked darn good bread, washed, milked, farmed, you name it. August said Frank did everything for him but have a baby, and he would have done that if he could."

Frank hated strangers. But he gradually unbent around Eugene, and sometimes even accompanied him on his hunting trips—pointing out good blinds and hard-to-spot cuts in the most tangled underbrush. He couldn't do any shooting because of his eye, but he was a good companion who knew how to keep silent. He and Eugene sometimes spent whole days together with no company but Eugene's hunting dogs. Both men were perfectly content not to say a word.

Bosh and Agnes's youngest child, Helen, grew up to be tall, big-boned, plain, and ungainly. She was more soft-spoken even than Eugene—except that in her case something always seemed to be stewing behind her silence, some grievance she wouldn't disclose. She hated to be noticed, detested being made fun of by her siblings, got red-faced and unintelligible whenever she was ever called on in class. She never talked back, but sometimes a sly, lemon-tart look crossed her face, as though she'd just thought of the snippiest comeback in the world but had too much self-regard to say it.

She had few friends, and only one who lasted—a girl named Irene, who lived across the train tracks in a house on First Avenue. Otherwise her main pleasure in life was the movies. There was a movie theater opposite the old town square (it had once been a burlesque house where Al Jolson and W. C. Fields had played), and Bosh took the whole family there every Saturday night. Bosh loved the comedies; sometimes as they walked home he would imitate Charlie Chaplin and make a mad silhouette against the night sky, twirling and prancing and kicking up clouds of dust from the road. But Helen was wild for exotic romances—*The Sheik* and *The Count of Monte Cristo*. She was inconsolable for weeks after Rudolph Valentino died.

For years it seemed as though graduating from high school was going to be Clarence's only accomplishment. Even with the diploma he had a hard time finding work. Just like his father, he went through a lot of jobs—so many that afterward the family couldn't remember them all. He did day labor at the radiator factory; he clerked at stores around town; and he spent one miserable winter trudging from door to door selling "real silk hosiery."

His best job was with a local passenger railroad. He sorted mail on the daily run between Saint Louis and Chicago. He knew nothing about either city when he started, and he never saw any more of them than their rail terminals. But day after day, as he looked up addresses in the battered street guides and shoved the envelopes into the pigeonholes labeled with the names of the branch post offices, he gradually built up mental images of the city grids—what ethnic names were clustered in what neighborhoods, which business districts were flourishing and which were getting dunned by mobs of creditors. He got to the point where he figured he could find his way around either city blindfolded without having set foot on a single street. So in the summer of 1926, he announced to Bosh and Agnes that he was moving to Chicago to try his luck there.

4

The Champion Distancer

THE HOUSE ON Second Avenue was always crowded. Besides
Bosh and Agnes and the flock of children, there was also a
floating population of visiting cousins, friends of friends, and
overnight guests who wouldn't leave. Bosh liked to keep up his
father's old tradition of hospitality: it was a rare meal where
fewer than a dozen people sat down at the dining room table.
At bedtime cots and mattresses were strewn over the floors of
every room, and on the hottest nights people moved out to the
back porch and the yard and sprawled like lions on the veldt.

The big occasion each week was Sunday dinner after
church. Everybody in the neighborhood had a standing invitation. Agnes cooked an enormous pot roast (the menu never
changed, even in the height of summer) and laid out heaping
bowls of side dishes: string beans in porked vinegar, moun-

tains of mashed potatoes and corn, gleaming ponds of corn relish, and clutches of fresh-baked biscuits. There were flagons of wine and pitchers of fresh milk and spiced lemonade; dessert was peach pie topped with cinnamon ice cream. When the weather was fine, everyone ate in the backyard, at long picnic tables draped with red-checked tablecloths beneath the thin shade of Bosh's peach orchard. Sometimes the freight trains came trundling past the back fence, trailing their squalls of cinders; the regulars became adept at hurriedly covering up bowls and platters with their napkins or with empty dishes. When the weather was cold or foul, everybody crowded around the heavy old table in the dining room, with the spillover at the kitchen table, and jokes were called back and forth through the open doorway. Toward twilight, if the sky was clear, everyone moved out to the front yard and sat together watching the lanterns of the wagons slowly bob through the dark along Troy Road.

In those days the southern edge of Edwardsville was creeping toward the house like a glacier. Across the tracks on First Avenue there was now a new row of bungalows; down the wandering dirt track on Second were a couple of sprawling houses and a poultry farm. Clapboard storefront buildings were springing up on Troy Road, bringing with them streetlights and electric lines. Bosh paid to have the house wired: a new pole drooping with a spaghetti tangle of cabling was planted just outside the picket fence, and soon Bosh was proudly showing each new visitor how every room in the house had its own outlet.

Bosh was a familiar figure around the neighborhood by then. Everybody up and down Troy Road recognized his gentle lope. Sometimes he dressed to the teeth and sauntered downtown to play pool, but he was always willing to stop and chat with new neighbors and passersby along the way, and frequently he'd throw away whatever he was planning to do that day and help someone out with a carpentry project or plumbing repair. He always surprised people with the thoroughness and quality of his work—especially if they'd observed him lolling about his own house like a pet dog. When the trains came by, Agnes and the children would race through the backyard rescuing sheets from the clotheslines, while Bosh would be seen dozing in his hammock under the back porch eave, sheltered from the hot black showers of cinders falling all around him.

When Prohibition came in, Bosh was the first in the neighborhood to take up winemaking. The bottles he brought up from his basement soon became the treasured high point of Sunday dinner. Everybody agreed he was an exceptional winemaker—though they couldn't help shaking their heads over the absurd flavors he insisted on bottling: dandelion, peach, blackberry, apricot. But he was surprisingly diffident about beer. He never bothered to make his own; like the rest of the neighborhood, he bought it at a corner tavern on Troy Road that languidly masqueraded as a laundry (men's long johns hung in the window, and a stack of shirt boxes hid the taps). Unlike everyone else, he didn't take the time to chill it.

"That was such terrible beer we had then," one of his neighbors told me. "Just dreadful. And then seeing Bosh drink it warm—imagine how that tasted!" It had been seventy-five years, but the memory still made her shudder.

The neighbors remembered Agnes, too. She was Bosh's keeper, the household's taskmaster, and the children's disciplinarian. She'd never much cared whether the children stayed in school—she was fond of saying that book learning never did anybody any good that she'd ever heard of. But she was determined that they be devout churchgoers. She'd never been happy pretending to be a Catholic, and a few years into the marriage she told Bosh she wanted the family to begin attending a newly built church of the Disciples of Christ.

Bosh agreed; he was indifferent to religion. But for Agnes it was a return to something deep and comforting. The Disciples of Christ had none of the somber rituals of the Catholic Church, nor the wilder goings-on typical of the Protestant churches in the deep country. Ranting, testifying, snake handling, speaking in tongues—to her this would all have been as strange as the witches' sabbaths in Bosh's stories. Instead the stress was right where she preferred it—on good fellowship, sensible obedience, and a clear conscience.

In the mid-1920s Bosh found a new extravagance: radio. The first battery-operated sets were appearing in Edwardsville's stores then—units that could be plugged into wall outlets were still a few years away. Bosh bought the fanciest model he could afford. You had to listen through headphones, and the only controls were two unmarked knobs that changed the frequency and the volume in unpredictable ways. Bosh spent hours hunched over it, twiddling the knobs and straining to make out anything at all through the undifferentiated roar of static.

Most of what he heard was wholly mysterious. There were horrible wailings and bellowings like demons caught in a thunderstorm, strange chirps and beeps of unknown provenance, and eerie jumbles of distorted music and voices from competing stations that were broadcasting on the same frequency. Only at rare intervals, as though in the lull of a gale, was there something recognizably human—a faint voice ranting a sermon, a lonely fiddle sawing out a fragmentary melody. Then the roaring drowned it out again, and no touch of the knobs, however patient or incremental, could recapture it.

There was a game popular among radio enthusiasts in those days that Bosh and a few of his friends began playing.

They would hang on to a recognizable broadcast, no matter what it was, until the announcer identified the call letters and location, and when they compared notes the next day, whoever had heard the most remote station was the winner. They called it "distancing," or "DX-ing"—"DX" was the ham radio code for "distance."

Distancing depended on the fluky way radio signals bounce off the ionosphere at night: a station a thousand miles away could briefly come in more clearly than one on the other side of town. Bosh and his friends mostly heard a scattering of broadcasts from around the heartland—backcountry music from Illinois and Missouri and Kentucky, down-home bands playing "Sail Away Ladies" or "Down the Old Plank Road." But sometimes they'd dimly catch jazz from Chicago or the somber boom of classical music from New York. And once, long after midnight, Bosh heard a tinkle of marimba music and a faint voice unmistakably announcing a broadcast from a ballroom in Havana, Cuba. That made Bosh, at least for a while, the town's champion distancer.

Clarence spent his first winter in Chicago living in a cheap rooming house on the Near North Side and working the occasional day labor at the big factories north and west of the Loop. The view from his room was of smokestacks and slag heaps along the slate-gray river and the unbroken overcast sky. He was miserably lonely.

One day he got a letter from home.

Edwardsville, Ill
Feb 7 1927

Dear Son

Well I guess you think that I have forgotten you because I don't write but you know your dad and I have poor eyes and can't see. I got your dad's glasses on now which he got from grandma but they don't fit my eyes very well. You'll have to excuse us both for not writing.

I thought if I would write you a letter once, maybe it will bring you good luck finding a job soon. I certainly feel sorry for you that you always have such bad luck. But hope you will soon find one. Work is very scarce here. Hilda came home yesterday. She gets home once a week but she wishes she could come home to stay it is so lonesome at grandma's. It sure is warm outside today. I guess there will be lots of sick. It is too warm for this time of the year. So take care of yourself that you don't get sick.

The radio is working pretty good but your dad won't have it so loud. Takes too much juice. Needs 3 new A batteries every 2 weeks. He sure enjoys it so what is the difference.

How are the cookies getting along or can't you eat them.

The roads in front of the house are awful poor, the worst I ever saw them.

Well, Clarence I see I am going uphill so you will have to excuse my writing. I never noticed it till I had this page half wrote.

News is scarce around here, besides I never go away. Well I hope this letter reaches you by February 9th and have a job by the time you are 24 years old. Please enclosed find 3 bucks for a happy birthday. 1 buck is from Hilda. She also wishes you a happy birthday and hope you have good luck for a new job.

Well I don't know any more new so I will hope that you have good luck which we all hope you have. Will close with love from all to you.

Answer soon
Mother

Shortly after that, Clarence's luck began to change. He got a job as a taxi driver. He still hadn't seen much of the city firsthand, but there were few applicants who knew the street grid as well as he did. And while he wasn't particularly skilled behind the wheel—most of his driving practice had been with a friend's pickup truck on the empty back roads around Edwardsville—that didn't turn out to be much of a handicap. The traffic in Chicago was a daylong paralysis of automobiles, trolley cars, trucks, and horse-drawn wagons; one more bad driver was hardly noticed.

The cab company worked the German neighborhoods

on the North Side. Clarence spent his shifts shuttling along Lincoln Avenue; it was a rare event when a passenger wanted to go as far as the Loop. Lincoln Avenue was where the German Catholics lived (the Protestants were mostly along Milwaukee Avenue to the west), and for Clarence it was like a vast dream-version of the old German community he remembered from his childhood. There were coffee shops and *fleischmarkts* and *brauhauses* and corner bakeries where English was never heard; there were pharmacies stocked with the latest in homeopathic and herbal remedies; there were newsstands bursting with arrays of Teutonic eccentricity (newspapers and magazines devoted to naturism and magnetic healing and national socialism); there were houses and storefronts and factory buildings with strange black turrets and spikes and battlements, like illustrations from a book of Gothic fairy tales.

Clarence decided to move there. He found a boardinghouse on Sacramento Avenue just off Irving Park. The owners were from Edwardsville, and they turned out to have known the Sehnerts slightly; they welcomed him in like the prodigal son.

The boardinghouse was on a quiet block of old brownstones—the sort of placid urban block where cats skittered safely between the rows of parked cars and kids played stickball and jump rope in the middle of the street. A few doors down was a big stoop where a group of young women gathered in the evenings. Clarence made a point of sauntering past them at the end of his shift. He was too shy to make eye contact. But he did quickly get the impression that one of them was deliberately positioning herself to watch him go by.

Her name was Mary Galambos. She had just turned twenty-three, which made her a year younger than Clarence. She was half German and half Hungarian. Her father had immigrated to Chicago from Budapest in the 1880s. He'd gotten a job at a German-language printing press on the North Side, been promoted several times, and ended up marrying the boss's daughter. Mary was their youngest child. She was small, plump, round-cheeked, and athletic. To Clarence she was as exotic as a Gypsy.

They took to strolling up and down Sacramento Avenue together in the evenings, under the watchful, mocking gaze of her friends. He told her a little about Edwardsville, and she pretended to be charmed—small-town life struck her as hopelessly dull. She described her life, and he didn't have to pretend to be enchanted. She was working that spring as a jockey at the little racetrack in Lincoln Park. He told her that he wanted to come see her race. She laughed and said not to bother; the races were fixed. Each morning a scary, stone-faced man from one of the North Side mobs came around to tell them the day's winners.

But Clarence came anyway. He rode the trolley car on his day off and joined the crowd at the rail to watch the horses thunder past. It was a gorgeous day. The grass was green, the trees were in flower, the sun played across the gray-and-brown mountain range of lakefront skyscrapers. He wasn't besotted enough to place any bets. But he did cheer wildly when Mary won the last race. She laughed when she saw him coming into the winner's circle to offer his congratulations.

Afterward they strolled through the park and the zoo. She talked about how beautiful and mysterious the park had been in her childhood—the fancy dress of the aristocrats, the clop of the horse-drawn carriages, the old trees shrouded in evening mist. Back then there had been skating on the lagoon in winter; a fully loaded beer wagon with a team of horses would be driven back and forth across it to test the ice. Clarence told her that his father had driven a beer wagon for years. They paused by the statue of Goethe at the north end of the park, and she was amused and appalled when he confessed he didn't know who Goethe was.

Clarence had never met anybody like Mary. She hadn't finished high school (she confided to him in dread secrecy), but she was determined to be cultured; she was forcing herself through a self-imposed literary boot camp and had just finished *Tom Jones* and was now starting on *Tristram Shandy*. Clarence was baffled by the idea of reading any book for pleasure, much less for status. Nor could he keep up with her whirl of opinions about current events; to him all the news was as remote as a war in China. But he was enchanted by her conversation even when—or mainly when—he had no idea what she was talking about.

He also responded well to her impatience and her ambition. From the first, she nagged at him about his job. It was high time, she informed him, that he quit driving a cab and find something respectable. Thinking of the stories he'd told her about sorting mail, she kept at him to apply for work at the Chicago post office. It took her months of needling persecution before he agreed. But at last he dragged himself downtown, and to his lifelong shock was immediately hired. After training at the behemoth main office, he was assigned to the new municipal airport just opening on the southwest side of town.

The airport was little more than a weedy lot about a mile square, with a couple of cinder runways, a row of hangars, and a makeshift terminal. Even on the busiest days no more than a dozen commercial airplanes took off or landed; they were mostly eight-seaters, and they each carried a couple of small sacks of mail. Sometimes hours went by with no motion anywhere inside or out. The wind socks hung limp on their tall vanes, the pilots and mechanics played poker in one of the hangars, and in the mail room Clarence dozed at his desk.

On his days off he spent every moment with Mary; they rode horses and went to the movies and talked in cafés for hours. Her family was Catholic, and he started attending mass at their parish church. (He didn't tell Agnes about that.) One late-summer evening they were walking along Clark Street when they were caught by a sudden squall. They ran for shelter and found themselves standing under the archway of the new Reebie building. The facade was an ornate terra-cotta mockup of an Egyptian temple—everything Egyptian was fashionable then, after the discovery of Tutankhamen's tomb. Clarence and Mary had just seen some foolish epic at the Biograph about the pharaohs. As the rain careened down around them, he kissed her and called her his Gypsy Cleopatra. A few weeks later he asked her to marry him.

The whole family came up from Edwardsville for the wedding. None of them had ever been in Chicago before, and when Clarence met them at Union Station they were huddled together like refugees. They were dazzled by his assurance as he led the way out into the streets. The scale of the city oppressed them, the interminable rows of brownstones and the furious bustle of the commercial districts. And they were intensely suspicious of Mary's family. Agnes in particular was in a black mood—the news had been broken to her that Clarence had converted to Catholicism for the ceremony.

The wedding reception was spread along most of the backyards of their block of Sacramento Avenue. It was a cool, clear day. White bunting draped the picnic tables, and white balloons jostled up from the fence gates. As the cloudless twilight came on, people lit up dozens of paper lanterns. Agnes and her daughters sat hunched together in a defensive knot, glaring at anyone forward enough to approach them; they kept casting worried glances at the city lights and the encircling brown-stones and the crisscrossing power lines as though they were under siege.

But Bosh was at his most exuberantly charming. He told jokes, offered toasts, and danced with his new in-laws. Afterward, people said it was a damn shame his friends back home couldn't have seen him. At the end of the evening, he gave Mary a special present, a gleaming brass horseshoe he'd cast at the foundry for her. "Always keep it with you for luck," he said, and Mary did.

For the rest of her life she could barely talk about him. "He was a wonderful man," she'd say, "just wonderful." And her eyes would fill with tears.

Soon after returning from Chicago, Bosh began to feel sick. He thought at first it was just bad digestion, the ordinary price of getting older. But he got steadily worse. His stomach burned constantly, and there was blood in his stool each morning. A couple of times without warning he doubled over in pain. He didn't believe in complaining; months went by before he said anything to Agnes, and months more before he nerved himself up to visit the doctor. The diagnosis was quick. He had colon cancer.

In the spring of 1929 he had to quit work and stay in bed. Friends and neighbors constantly came by to keep him company, and the house took on the air of a permanent, desultory party. He tried to rouse himself each Sunday to preside at the dinner table—but by summer he was too weak and the dinners came to an end. After the neighbors had to stop coming to the house, they went on helping in discreet ways. When Helen was on her way home from school somebody might lean out over a fence or from a kitchen window and invite her for dinner; that was a code letting her know that she shouldn't go home.

By the end of summer Bosh was on his last legs. The doctor was paying a house call when Agnes, in a fit of fury, demanded he do something. The doctor burst out that he was helpless, unless she wanted him to stick a red-hot poker up Bosh's rear to burn the tumor out. From the next room they heard Bosh weakly calling out that they shouldn't bother—he felt as though they'd already done it.

The doctor prescribed opium. But by then it would have taken a lethal dose to dent the pain. Instead, Bosh began asking his few permitted visitors, with a great show of conspiratorial whispering, if they could smuggle him bottles of peach brandy.

In the end, only Agnes could bear to be in the house for very long. She sat at the bedside, talking to Bosh about whatever came into her head. Sometimes she prayed—but Bosh just rolled his eyes and smiled. Sometimes she sang to him. Mostly she talked about their children—about how Clarence was doing in Chicago, and whether he and Mary would make them grandparents soon, or about some crazy thing Cecil had said to Pearl, or about how Hilda had grown so much more responsible staying with Franciska, or about whether Eugene and Helen would ever stop being so shy.

Bosh would appear to listen, though his gaze wandered off and he stared vaguely at the sunlight on the wallpaper. Those were his good days. On his bad days his screams were so loud they could be heard by the crews of the passing trains.

5

We Can't Take Care of Our Own

BOSH DIED IN October 1929. Agnes was left in a bad way. The doctor bills had cleaned her out, and she hadn't had a paying job since her days as a chambermaid at Sehnert's Hotel almost thirty years before. She knew that the family would do what it could to help her. But she also knew that the main burden was going to fall on her two children still living at home, Helen and Eugene. That didn't bother Agnes a bit. She took it for granted that children should support their parents—even if it meant putting their own lives aside permanently.

Helen was sixteen then, and just starting her junior year in high school. She was determined to graduate, because that was what Bosh had wanted. But Agnes informed her that further schooling was out of the question. So Helen dropped out and got a job as a seamstress at a local dressmaker. (She was hired through her aunt Daisy, who had been working there for several years, ever since she'd lost her husband to cancer.)

Helen had no particular talent for the job. She was clumsy with her hands, and she hated the interminable hours and painful difficulty of the work. But she never complained—not to her employers, not to Daisy, and especially not to Agnes. She remained bitter, though, for the rest of her life. Almost seventy years later, she was still saying how unjust it was that she'd had to quit school. "I was the best speller in my class," she said proudly, "and the best out-loud reader. And it was surprising, as I was the shy, reserved kind."

But things may have been even tougher on Eugene. He was eighteen, and with Clarence away in Chicago, he thought it his duty to be the man of the house. One of his father's old friends at the Nelson factory got him a job as a laborer in the porcelain shop. But that lasted only a couple of months. Nelson was doing badly that winter, and all their new hires were soon laid off. Eugene worked briefly as a handyman. After that he stood in line at the local factories each morning, only to be told there was no work.

By spring he was hopping trains to nearby towns and looking for day labor. Now and then he did pick up a few bucks—but that barely paid for his meals, and he was having to travel farther and farther for less and less of a return. So one night in early spring he told Agnes and Helen he didn't want to be a burden on them any longer; he was heading out on the road and wouldn't be back until he'd earned enough to pay for his keep. The next morning he was gone.

Over the spring of 1930, Agnes and Helen got used to having the house to themselves. They settled into a routine. They slept together in the big brass bed—Agnes couldn't bear to be alone in it at night. Each morning Helen walked to work at the dressmaker, while Agnes stayed at home and did the cooking and cleaning. She'd always been a good cook, and she liked to keep a spotless house. On weekends Hilda came home from her grandmother Franciska's house on Brown Street, and they opened up a foldout cot for her in the master bedroom.

Bored with life on Brown Street, Hilda wanted to enjoy her brief spells of freedom. She coaxed Helen into going with her to the roller-skating rink on Saturday evenings—that was where all their old school friends gathered. But Helen never liked skating; she was too shy and too clumsy. Whenever she had a choice she went to the movies instead. Hilda wanted her to be more social than that and even went so far as to locate a potential date for her. Helen approached Agnes for permission to go to the rink with this man—chaperoned by Hilda, of course. Agnes said absolutely not. Helen was furious, but she acquiesced. She didn't mention men or dating again for years.

That summer, Pearl and Cecil announced they were expecting their first child. They were around the house on Second Avenue a lot in those days, doing what they could to help Agnes cope. Cecil was an especially welcome presence. He was the only man left: Bosh was gone, Clarence was in Chicago, and there had been no word from Eugene in months. Cecil took upon himself all the heavy tasks. As autumn came, he hauled the coal and stocked wood for the stove and laid in the staple goods—big sacks of flour and sugar and coffee. He also kept the house riled up with his incessant teasing. He was especially rough with Helen. He liked to tell her that she had to get out from under Agnes's thumb before she soured into a lemony old maid.

The autumn was warm and wet, and Troy Road and Second Avenue were rivers of mud. Helen slogged off to work each day in high boots as though she were going swamp wading. (She had to walk up Troy Road a half mile to where the pavement began, and she rode the trolley car the rest of the way into town.) One December morning after she'd left and Cecil had set out in his pickup truck to the general store, Agnes and Pearl started in on a big job: cleaning out the stovepipes in the kitchen. Pearl was standing on a chair rehanging the last section of pipe when her water broke.

The labor was brief. Cecil was barely back from the store when the baby was born. They all knew immediately that something was wrong. The baby didn't emerge red faced and furious but silent and pale as wax. The cord was wrapped around her neck. For the rest of her life, Pearl believed that hanging the stovepipes was what did it.

Cecil took care of everything. He drove off again in the pickup truck and came back an hour later with a little wooden box and a lacy white blanket. It was still the middle of the day; Helen wasn't back from work yet, and Pearl was too weak to move. Cecil and Agnes went together to the old Catholic cemetery where the Sehnerts had their family plot, and he dug a little grave next to Bosh's headstone. In those days you needed no ceremony or official record to bury anyone—certainly not a stillborn. But the cemetery's director did happen to come by and asked for formality's sake what the baby's name was. That was something they hadn't discussed. But Cecil spoke up.

"Helen," he said.

A few weeks later, on a murky evening of heavy snow, Agnes saw someone coming through the back gate by the outhouse. She was about to get the shotgun when she recognized the silhouette: Eugene. As he shrugged out of his coat and shook off the snow, he was revealed to be both gaunt and muscular; his clothes were ragged, his hands were calloused, and he was so suntanned he was almost black.

He wouldn't say anything about where he'd been. He seemed, if possible, even quieter than when he'd left. At mealtimes he sat sullen and hunched, with his arm around his plate as though someone were going to steal his food. He was also broke. He had nothing to show for his months on the road but a couple of dollars. Agnes paid him a quarter a day to haul the coal and keep the furnace stoked—enough pocket change to buy cigarettes and the occasional beer.

On weekends he headed over to Alhambra to visit his uncles August and Frank. Sometimes he helped with chores or went hunting with them in the deep recesses of the countryside. Occasionally the three would drive out to a woodland crossroads and take a snow-buried track to an isolated farmhouse hidden in the trees. That was the local brothel. Eugene gladly spent what was left of his money there. But the rest of the time he was ill at ease and bored. As soon as the spring thaw came, he was off on the road again.

As 1931 ended, Franciska died in the old house on Brown Street. Her death came on Christmas Eve—she'd survived J.L. by one day short of twenty-six years. Hilda moved back into the house on Second Avenue, and the children divided up the furniture and sold the property. They couldn't have picked a worse time and they got a rock-bottom price. But by then they were grateful for every penny.

Pearl and Cecil left town the following year. He was out of a job: the Nelson company had gone under. But Cecil didn't stay idle long. He heard from his family that a small farm belonging to one of his uncles had lost its tenants and was standing empty. The farm was outside the town of Bourbonnais, on the other side of the state. Cecil immediately took Pearl there and settled into the farming life.

That same year the old coal mine up the tracks was shut down. Its abandoned equipment was hauled away to the scrap yard, and when the cold weather came the neighbors tore apart the derelict buildings for firewood. Then there was nothing left but a slag heap that had spontaneously combusted a few years earlier (it would go on smoldering for another thirty years). Farther on was the brick factory, running half shifts and often idle for weeks at a time. Toward town was the Nelson company, now shuttered, its whitewashed walls peeling and its skylight windows broken. Its utopian workers' village had been absorbed into Edwardsville—in exchange for accepting its laws and police, the villagers got a sewer system and electricity.

In town, there were long rows of boarded-up businesses. Helen's job with the dressmaker vanished and she never found out why; she arrived one morning to find the place padlocked and the owner gone. After that she could get only day labor at a local shirt factory. Then she joined the Garment Workers' Union, and they occasionally found piecework for her.

In the spring and summer of 1933, there were big parades through town celebrating the new National Recovery Administration. The NRA's symbol—a blue eagle with the motto "We Do Our Part"—began appearing in store windows. (It meant that the store owner had agreed to pay a minimum wage.) The NRA brokered a deal between the clothing industry and the Garment Workers' Union, and Helen got called in for steady work at a dress factory in Saint Louis. After years of scrounging, she was bringing home fifteen dollars a week. It seemed to her like a miracle. She was always fiercely prounion after that; the old employees called her the NRA baby.

During those years, Hilda and Helen and Agnes were better off than almost anybody they knew. They had something worth its weight in gold: a house owned free and clear. Bosh had paid off the mortgage, and the property was still in an unincorporated area where the taxes (and services) were negligible. They had a big vegetable garden, fruit trees, and a chicken coop. The money that Helen brought home was more than enough to buy the basics—milk, meat, flour, and coffee. Helen even had change left over for the movies. Things were tougher in the winter, when Eugene was home and there was an extra mouth to feed. But even if he arrived with empty pockets, he was willing to do all the hard labor around the house for cigarette money. And besides, he was always gone in the spring.

When Eugene went on the bum, all he had to do was walk along the railroad tracks. About a half a mile down from the house was a little copse by a stream where a hobo jungle had sprung up. It was a cluster of lean-tos and tents and collapsing sheds around a patch of trampled ground. The jungle would start to empty out whenever one of the big trains approached. It was tense, jumping a train. Everyone had to stay hidden in the trees until the last moment to be sure no railroad bulls were watching. Then they'd dash forward and lunge at an open boxcar door, or the ladder on the side of a coal hopper, or a stray rope dangling from the cargo lashed to a flatcar—anything at all to get on board before the train cleared the curve and picked up speed on its way west.

The train ran through open country for several miles and then gradually lost itself within the old, decaying network of spur lines and abandoned industrial strips on the Illinois side of the Mississippi. Across the wide, gray waters was cinder-brown Saint Louis, perpetually wreathed in smoke. Eugene would usually make his first stop there; he found temporary shelter in one of the countless sprawling shantytowns that had flowered in the city's vacant lots and derelict factory grounds. "Hoovervilles," they were called, in honor of the president.

The biggest Hooverville in Saint Louis was alongside one of the train yards. It covered nearly a square mile and had a population of several thousand: more people were huddled there than in the whole town of Edwardsville. But Eugene rarely stayed more than a night or two. It was a squalid, loud, chaotic place, filled with the stench of open sewage and the smoke of countless trash-can fires. Toward dawn each day there would be a general exodus as people swarmed out to join the lines snaking to the big soup kitchens or to the few factory gates around town that weren't already hung with No Jobs signs. Eugene didn't bother with any of that, after a first few tries. Instead, he sauntered along the tracks until he could catch a likely-looking outbound freight train, destination anywhere.

Most of what he found on his travels was just like what he'd left behind. Wherever the trains passed, he saw the homeless sleeping in every park and town square. Cities had armed guards posted at their dumps to prevent people from scavenging them for food. Vagrancy was a felony in much of the country: an encounter with the wrong cop or the wrong judge could earn you a couple of years on a chain gang. Some towns, meaning to be kind, put up huge warning billboards along their main roads and by their rail yards that read *Homeless Men Keep Moving—We Can't Take Care of Our Own.*

Eugene mainly stuck to the rail lines west of the Mississippi. The land there still looked barely settled. The coal towns along the Rockies and the lumber towns in the immense virgin pine forests of the Pacific Northwest were separated by endless reaches of desolation; days would pass, and all Eugene would see would be the occasional ill-defined dirt road, or a long line of fence posts along a distant hilltop, or a grain elevator sitting on the horizon like a tower in a fairy tale. During the dust-bowl years, the desert had spread into the heartland;

the trains passed through wastelands that had once been cultivated fields but where derelict farmhouses were now half-
buried in blown topsoil. Once he watched a dust storm billow
across the prairie. It was like a sickly thunderstorm of yellow,
brown, and black, and when the fringes of it passed across the
tracks, the train was engulfed in furious dust that stung like a
cloud of wasps.

He was never comfortable riding the rails. But he did get
used to it eventually. The hoboes had figured out every single place on a moving train where a human being could fit.
Eugene tried them all at one time or another—from the high
heaps of coal in the hopper cars to the big rods beneath the
flatcars that skimmed just a few inches above the rail beds.

Boxcars were the best rides. But you had to pick them
carefully. If you were too close to the engine you could get
caught in a shower of live cinders that might put out an eye
or scar you for life. Eugene got into the habit—learned from
the longtime hoboes—of riding with a rag tied across his face.
There were other dangers. The cinders sometimes set fire to
the heaps of straw where the hoboes slept. Then, too, a good
safe boxcar, one toward the caboose, was usually crowded, and
riders could be murderous in defending it.

Sometimes there was no choice but to climb up onto the
boxcar roof. That was the most dangerous spot of all, particularly on long, lulling night journeys. There was nothing
to hold on to if you dozed off and started to slip. That didn't

keep anyone from riding there, though. One of the most common sights of those years, seen everywhere the railroads ran, was a freight train bearing a single-file line of travelers on its back, like the fins of an enormous lizard.

In the old times, the hoboes had had their own language and their own mythology—a secret world of Okies and bindle stiffs, of John Henry and Boxcar Bertha and the emperor of the North Pole. Some of that was still current when Eugene went on the bum. Sometimes people in the hobo jungles passed an idle evening singing the old songs, and sometimes a firebrand from the Wobblies would give a political speech (there were Hoovervilles where a red Wobbly membership card was required for admission), and always there was the chatter about what city might have work, where the local cops and the railroad bulls were most vindictive, what you'd do if you got to Easy Street.

But the traditional hobo culture was being washed out by a flood of undifferentiated misery. There were millions of homeless people in those years, and few had any use for the romance of the open road. Nor did they go in much for camaraderie. You were never asked where you were from and how you'd ended up on the bum. People shied away from that because of the implication that your hard times were your fault. Everybody kept their distance. Anyway, it was hard to open up and make friends, because life was too chancy. If your hand slipped as you jumped for a coal-hopper ladder, or you lost your balance as you clung to a boxcar roof on a mountain curve—then in the blink of an eye you were separated from a newfound friend forever.

Eugene followed the great tides of migrant and seasonal labor around the West. He got road work and construction work. He logged in the summers and worked farms at harvesttime. One year he spent a month in Nevada, the site of Boulder Dam, the great federal project of those years. But he couldn't stick it out. The men slept in a tent city in a waterless canyon below the construction site, and the temperatures at night rarely went below the mid-nineties.

His best job came later that summer, when he worked as a field hand at a big farm in northern California. The owner was impressed enough with his dedication to keep him on as a handyman after the harvest. He slept in a bunkhouse and got three square meals a day. One of the other hands had signed up for a correspondence-school course in electrical work; after he dropped the books in impatient incomprehension, Eugene picked them up and read them cover to cover. He did so mostly out of boredom; the payoff came months later, when he lucked into another big construction job, and he could understand what the electricians were doing. He found that he had the beginnings of a trade.

Each year, as the fall ended and the snow line began creeping down out of Canada, he joined the general migration south. By the time of the first hard freezes in the Midwest, he'd reached a familiar hobo jungle in a strip of woodland along a railroad junction. There'd usually be a few other travelers lingering there. They had a fire going in a corroded trash can and a mulligan stew simmering; someone would lug a battered bucket down to the creek for water, and when the stew was edible somebody else would rouse the sleepers huddled in the lean-tos.

Then the sound of an approaching train would come rumbling through the frosty air. There'd be that familiar flurry in the jungle: everyone staked a place along the tracks to make their jump. Eugene always made as if to join them—but he'd hang back unobtrusively until the caboose sailed past. Then he was alone. He'd saunter down the spur line that led out of the forest. Past the trees was a tangle of low shabby roofs and chicken coops and outhouses and tumbled wire fences. People wouldn't look twice at a hobo walking along the tracks there; nobody noticed when he turned aside and vanished through the back gate of his home.

J.L. Sehnert, around 1900

Franciska Sehnert, around 1900

Sehnert's Hotel in Edwardsville in 1900

Bosh and Agnes with Clarence and Oliver in 1905

The house soon after it was built

Bosh in 1922

Clarence and Mary on the road in 1927

Helen and Hilda, around 1930

Eugene, sometime in the 1930s

Dorothy, Nancy, and Bob in Edwardsville, Easter 1943

Hilda and Marty in 1944

Helen and Hilda in 1947

Helen at her sewing machine

6

The World Doesn't Owe You a Living

ONE NIGHT IN the winter of 1937, John Galambos, my grandmother Mary Sehnert's father, stayed out late at his favorite tavern. The tavern was one of those corner places that were scattered through the residential neighborhoods on the North Side of Chicago: a dark storefront on an elm-arched side street, marked by a cluster of small neon signs in the window, like the magic words in a fairy tale—*Blatz, Pabst, Hamm's, Schlitz*. The tavern's interior was dank and somnolent. The regulars nodded at the bar like shaggy toadstools. For whole evenings, the only noise was the buzz of a boxing match on the radio. John could spend hours there undisturbed, alternating beer and peppermint schnapps.

That particular night he exited into a snowstorm. The sidewalks were deserted and the windows of the brownstones were dark. He launched himself across Irving Park Road in the middle of the block and had almost reached the other side when a car came roaring out of the glittery murk and hit him. He landed in a bank of ice and snow between two parked cars. Fresh snow gradually covered him over. In the morning, somebody noticed the weird shape in the snowbank and the frozen blood trailing down toward the pavement. The driver of the car was never identified.

John's widow, Eva, couldn't bear to stay in Chicago. She moved to Arizona to live with her sister. The family brownstone passed to her daughter Mary and Mary's husband, Clarence. They had been living with their children on the Southwest Side, near the municipal airport, where Clarence worked. But Clarence gladly accepted the commute to and from Ravenswood for the chance to be a home owner.

Clarence and Mary had three children: my mother, Dorothy; my uncle Bob; and my aunt Nancy. They grew up as classic Chicago neighborhood kids. They knew every side street and alley in Ravenswood and remained absolutely blank about the city beyond. The family did its shopping at the big commercial district at Belmont and Ashland, and on summer nights rode the streetcars down Western Avenue to Riverview; the kids went to double features at the movie palaces on Irving Park Road and drank their phosphates and root-beer floats at the drugstore fountains on Lawrence. Dorothy doesn't remember ever traveling as far from home as the Loop before she was a teenager.

It was a world wholly enclosed by the low, steeple-spiked skyline. Within its maze of ancient brownstones the kids played jump rope and jacks beneath endless corridors of elms. The leaf canopy was so tightly interwoven the streets were like twilight at high noon. Dorothy remembers you could walk for a block during a summer thunderstorm without feeling a raindrop. Everywhere the kids went, they were watched over by an unobtrusive network of neighborhood monitors: flocks of clucking hausfraus and idle men sitting in front of lodges and social clubs. Anybody odd or unknown or threatening would set off warning bells in bakeries and cafés and butcher shops and *brauhauses* all over the North Side.

The Sehnert home itself was dark and stifling, like every other home in their neighborhood. Clarence and Mary kept it as it had been in her father's time. There were overstuffed armchairs and tasseled lamp shades, prints of Hungarian country scenes on the walls and a row of painted beer steins on the mantel. Nor was it enlivened by Clarence and Mary themselves. They were stern parents, neither unloving nor indulgent. They expected obedience from their children and they got it; they didn't much care about child rearing otherwise. Dorothy says she can't remember a single time in her childhood when her family did anything relaxed and companionable, even sit around the kitchen table and laugh.

Clarence did all right by his family financially, even in

the worst years. But he had become a diffident, secretive man. He took over the basement and turned it into his workroom, and he spent every available moment hidden away there, carving or drilling or lathing or sanding. He was never happier than when he was fitting together the dowels of a rebuilt chair. He was affectionate toward the children at times. But his affection tended to emerge in oblique and ineffectual ways. One autumn he disappeared from their lives entirely, only to reemerge at Christmas with a gift from Santa: a fantastically carved miniature zoo where they could keep all their toy animals. When he was present, he tended to be taciturn and abrupt. He thought his main duty as a parent was to enforce Mary's orders. To this end he manufactured a series of handmade paddles for Mary's use in disciplining the children— and long afterward, when the children were all grown and married, he presented each of them with a paddle for the disciplining of his grandchildren.

Mary was quick-witted, hot tempered, and unsympathetic. Her ideas of parenting boiled down to "Spare the rod and spoil the child" and "Children should be seen and not heard"— maxims she would repeat with firmness and immense good humor, as though savoring the misery they caused her kids. But she was also determined that they be clever and literate. She bought a set of classic illustrated novels and required the kids to read chapters aloud to one another every night. They made their halting way through *Treasure Island* (their favorite) and *Northwest Passage* (a bore) and Howard Pyle's *King Arthur* (too hard to read, but the illustrations were magical). Sometimes Clarence hung back in the doorway and listened, and though he'd never read a book in his life, he found himself rooting for Jim Hawkins and sneakily admiring Long John Silver.

Mary enjoyed laying down the law to the kids about what the world was like and what they should expect from it. "The world doesn't owe you a living," she was fond of saying. Other times she'd say, "It's a cold world out there." She was nominally Catholic—at least, she took the children to mass every Sunday—but she had no interest in Christian doctrine and was particularly scornful of the idea of charity. "Anybody who'd take a handout," she'd say, "is the lowest of the low." During the years of the Great Depression she regarded the swarms of homeless and destitute as object lessons for her children: the trash-can scavengers and the somber-faced sleepers in the parks were layabouts who'd brought their troubles on themselves.

But that's not to say Mary was cold. She was passionate— but only about Clarence. This made them the subject of endless gossip around Ravenswood. Everybody watched them with a kind of astonishment, as though there were something unnatural about a husband and wife so much in love. Even their children shook their heads about it fifty and sixty years later. They'd always known they weren't even in the running for their parents' affection. Dorothy says that all her life when she thought about a warm and loving family, what she pictured was the house in Edwardsville.

It was their annual expedition: as soon as school let out for the year, Clarence and Mary would take the kids down to Edwardsville and leave them there for the summer. Then they went off alone together.

They invariably set out right at dawn on a day in early June. By midmorning they were out of the city and headed southwest on Route 66—the great "mother road of America" that cut diagonally across Illinois and swept on through the heartland and the southwest to California. In those days it was notorious for its awful traffic. Wrecked and abandoned cars were heaped on its shoulders; the billboards were so thick on either side that the landscape for miles at a time was blotted out. Sometimes they'd top a rise and see nothing ahead but a motionless, hooting double column of cars, trucks, buses, and tractors stretching all the way out to the green horizon.

They never reached Edwardsville before dark. There was always a big party to welcome the children for their summer stay, with the whole neighborhood invited. But Clarence and Mary were usually so restless to get back on the road, they wouldn't even stick around through dinner. Today, asked where her parents went, Dorothy expels a long, slow sigh and says, "I have absolutely no idea." Nancy laughs and says, "God knows."

The first sound the kids heard in the morning was the squall and squeak of the hand pump just outside the kitchen door. Hilda was beginning the day by drawing a bucket of water. The kids lingered in bed, watching the leaf-dappled sunlight spread across the ceiling and seep down the floral wallpaper. More sounds came to them: skillets banging, the cat-hiss sizzle of melting butter, the clunk of plates on a tablecloth. And meanwhile muffled voices were rising from the master bedroom—Agnes and Helen were awake and quarreling. Then Hilda barged into the room and demanded to know whether the kids were going to lollygag in bed all morning.

Breakfast was a hurried affair, because Helen was always running late: she barely had time to gulp down the scalded coffee and tear apart a sweet roll smeared with Hilda's peach preserves before she was out the door. Then Agnes settled in her rocking chair, Hilda began clearing the kitchen table, and the day began.

They always thought of Hilda as the perfect surrogate mother. She was constantly fussing over them, cooking special treats for them, thinking up games for them to play, and assigning them chores if they made the mistake of looking bored. She regarded it as a special privilege to help her wash the dishes—she'd set the honored one on a stool beside her and solemnly hand over plates to dry. Sometimes she gathered everyone in a circle in the shade of the backyard on the hottest days and had them peeling peaches for preserves or snipping green beans. Occasionally unlucky neighbors would get roped in, and Hilda would come bustling out with a tray of lemonade glasses before clucking with disapproval over their sloppy work.

Every Saturday afternoon she'd drag a big galvanized tub into the middle of the kitchen floor and fill it with buckets of hot water boiled on the stove. She'd watch over Dorothy and Nancy as they scrubbed, and offer peremptory commands for places missed (she withdrew discreetly to the backyard when it was Bob's turn). The next morning she'd dress them for church and pinch them for the dirt they'd managed to accumulate overnight. "Being around her," one of my relatives remembers, "was like drowning in love."

But the kids felt closest to Helen. She was the youngest in the household—only seventeen years older than Dorothy. She was much more relaxed around them than she was around adults. She lost all her shyness and joined in all their games. She'd get a sly, crafty grin on her face when she won, as though nobody could know how deep her pleasure ran. She seemed magically attuned to their feelings—particularly when it came to public embarrassment. One summer she taught them to roller-skate by clearing a practice space in the basement, where none of the neighbor kids could see them take a fall.

She was also the one who'd uncomplainingly get out of bed in the middle of the night to take the girls to the outhouse, and she'd always sit on the second seat and keep them company. "That was our time for exchanging confidences," Dorothy remembers.

Agnes was more aloof. "Hilda and Helen doted on her," Nancy says, "but none of the kids ever got to know her." She remained in her rocking chair in the dining room bay. If she started up to try to help with something—a pot boiling over, or laundry left on the line as a train approached—Hilda would furiously shush her back to her place, like a mother hen corralling an escaped chick. She did rouse herself once a week for church, which was her main pleasure in life. The preacher was as gnarled as an old oak and his voice was like two branches rubbing together, but Agnes loved the way he'd work up a fury denouncing the enemies of America: Catholics, Jews, Freemasons, and Communists.

Mostly the children were on their own. Each day Hilda scooted them out of the house after breakfast, and they were sometimes out till sundown exploring the neighborhood. They were particularly fond of the landscape along the railroad corridor. Toward town the tracks led past the abandoned coal mine; they sometimes found fresh footprints in the dirt outside or boards pried from its sinister entrance, warnings that hoboes had taken shelter there. On rainy days they dared one another to get as close as they could to the smoldering slag heap, until they could hear it hissing like a nest of snakes.

Farther on was the brick factory, and around its back were huge hills of sand. The sand had been brought by barge up the Mississippi from the Gulf of Mexico, and it sparkled with constellations of seashells. The kids could spend hours there, whooping and yelling and sliding down the slopes until a security guard heard the racket and chased them off.

In the other direction the tracks led into the woods. Sometimes the kids could summon up the nerve to venture there. Deep within the trees was the hobo jungle, and if any of its denizens spotted them the kids would bolt in hilarious terror, screaming the old jump-rope rhyme "Hobo, hobo, where have you been?"

At twilight the kids would wait by the front fence for Helen to come home from work in Saint Louis. She'd turn the corner bedraggled and weary, but when she saw them she'd immediately brighten and hurry the last few steps home. Sometimes she brought presents for Nancy, the youngest child: doll clothes she'd secretly sewn from the scraps of fine fabric left over from her shift. Before dinner she and the kids would sit together on the front porch and play a game they'd invented called "Movie Stars." As the twilight sky dimmed, each time a new star appeared someone would call out the initials of some actor or actress, and Helen would have to guess who it was. She proved to be invincible at it. If anyone said "C.G.," she seemed to know by telepathy whether it was Cary Grant or Clark Gable.

Then everyone gathered around the enormous old dining

table for dinner. Agnes said grace. She always included a prayer for her son Eugene, wherever he was on his travels—that was the only time the kids ever heard him mentioned. After dinner came the washing up; the kids were expected to handle the towel drying and the placement of dishes in the drainer with solemn dignity. Then Hilda cleared the yellowed linen cloth from the table and everyone returned to their places to play cards. The windows were opened to the night air, and countless moths batted at the screens.

Sometimes toward bedtime the kids would hear the first gnawing grumbles of thunder as a big storm came over the Mississippi. Soon the rain would be bombarding the roof and hurtling down the gutters and tumbling out into the hedges. Afterward the children would lie awake and listen to the slow return of ordinary night sounds: the rustling of the trees, the sigh and roar of traffic on Troy Road, and the remote thunk of a steeple clock. And sometimes, long after midnight, a long caravan of boxcars and tanker cars and flatcars and hopper cars would come creaking down the tracks, and the house would slowly fill up with an immensity of sound as mournful and comforting as the sea.

Helen always set off to work with a movie magazine in her purse. That was a concession to her mother's sense of propriety: Agnes didn't allow those sorts of magazines in the house, and Helen had to keep them out of sight. (Agnes didn't actually approve of women reading anything; she thought no good could come of a woman getting educated.) Helen waited until she was on the train before turning to the latest—whether Bette Davis or Paulette Goddard would get the lead in *Gone with the Wind*, or whether Ruth Etting would be able to escape her disastrous marriage to that shady New York mobster Moe the Gimp.

The train took her through the industrial zones and working-class neighborhoods east of the river, then across the wide, barge-crowded water into Saint Louis. In those years she worked at a succession of high-end dress manufacturers in the garment district. She didn't bother to keep track of them. Her loyalty was to the union and she didn't care where they sent her. Sometimes she got lucky and spent a long spell in a modern, federally approved factory, the kind with ventilation and sunlight. Even better was one with big windows that could be opened to the air on sweltering summer afternoons. Other times she was consigned to purgatorial ovens with bolts of fabric in mountainous heaps and air thick with floating threads and tufts of cotton.

But in any case she always returned home each day so tired she could barely move. Sometimes she would rouse herself to walk across the train tracks and visit her friend Irene, who was also unmarried and who lived with her family on First Avenue. But most nights after dinner she would sit at the dining table, listening to the radio and dealing out game after game of solitaire. The radio was in the parlor, so she would listen to it through the open door; the parlor was reserved for guests and she never felt right sitting in there by herself. She liked soap operas like *Amanda of Honeymoon Hill* and *Mary Noble, Backstage Wife*—anything where the heroine was long-suffering and where happiness stayed out of reach.

Then it was bedtime. She settled in each night next to her mother. Agnes was a heavy sleeper and often snored; Helen tossed and turned through the night, seething at the noise Agnes was making. They wore heavy nightgowns even in the summertime; on all but the coldest mornings they woke up sweaty, miserable, and snappish.

Before Helen left for work, she combed out her mother's waist-length hair. Agnes submitted with bad grace. She used the time to denounce Helen's attitude. Helen had a knack for getting on Agnes's nerves. She seemed to know just which brand of patent medicine would be most exasperatingly wrong, and which brand of soap most stung the skin, and how to put off errands until the last nerve-racking moment before the stores closed. Helen listened submissively. But when Agnes went on too long, she'd fling the comb against the wall in a fury and stalk out of the room.

Her life had no obvious opportunities for adventure. But over the winter of 1939, she met someone. Nobody in the family ever knew his name. He was just a man who struck up a conversation with her at a Sunday-evening church dance, where she had gone to keep Hilda company. A week or two later she bumped into him again when they were standing in line at a movie theater. And a few days after that, they met for lunch surreptitiously in Saint Louis, at a drugstore counter amid the tumult of the noon rush. They looked prim, shy, and uncomfortable, for all the world like a minister and a church secretary discussing an awkward detail regarding the next week's service. But for Helen it was the most exciting moment of her life, because he was married.

Somehow Agnes found out. Maybe Helen had let something slip to Hilda, who then turned around and informed Agnes on her. Or somebody in town spotted them, and the word came to Agnes over the back fence with the laundry-day gossip. In any event it roused her to a fury no one had seen in years. She confronted Helen and told her to break it off immediately. Ragingly defiant, Helen said she and her beloved were going to be married. Agnes said she would never agree, and she told Helen it was a daughter's duty to obey her mother. Helen, attaining a clarity of anger that Bette Davis or Joan Crawford might have envied, swore that in that case she would never again mention men or marriage as long as she lived.

Things went back to normal after that. Helen resumed her daily commute into the city. As each day's shift began, she bent over in her long-familiar hunch of pain. Her back ached, her legs cramped, her shoulders creaked in their old agony, and the tendons in her hands were aflame. Then the roar of the sewing machines drowned out every thought in her head.

7

War Fever

THE NIGHT AFTER Pearl Harbor was attacked, there was a torchlight procession through the streets of Edwardsville and a rally in the town square. The speakers exhorted the men of the town to enlist. The next day, lines of young men snaked out from the recruitment offices, and all the passersby were stopping to shake their hands. The lines were longer the next day, and the day after that; pretty soon any able-bodied man in civilian clothes found himself harassed on the street by neighbors demanding to know why he wasn't in uniform.

Eugene watched the fever sweep through Edwardsville with a brooding lack of interest. He'd only recently come back to town for good after years on the bum, and he still moved around the streets like a stranger. Even at home he was an elusive presence. He kept to himself and would not

discuss his time on the road. He fixed up the attic as a bedroom and furnished it with an ornate brass bed he'd found at
a junkyard. He forbade anybody else to go up there. At the
dinner table he kept his head down and rarely spoke. When
I asked people who'd known him in those years for a sample
of his conversation, all anybody could think of was, "Pass the
potatoes."

He'd lucked into a job—he was an electrician's helper at
the enormous Shell Oil refinery in Wood River, a few miles
northwest of Edwardsville on the Mississippi. The refinery
was in a frenzy of expansion and was hiring every man with
the feeblest hint of training or experience. But Eugene wasn't
sure how long it would last. Like every other man in Edwardsville, he'd registered for the draft, and he expected to be called
up at any moment. But the weeks and months passed with no
summons. When he finally appeared before the draft board,
he was told that his job at the refinery was critically important
war work and he was exempt from military service. That was
fine by him. He went back home.

Eugene spent his free time tramping around the deep
countryside with his hunting dogs. He kept two of them then:
a regal, dignified mutt named Bingo and a testy collie named
Poochie who was Helen's darling—the first in a long series of
mean, unlovable dogs that she doted on. He might have passed
the whole war with no company but the dogs if it hadn't been
for his sister Hilda's new boyfriend.

Around the corner from the family house on Troy Road was a grocery called Wehrle's. It was a little storefront of gray clapboard with a painted Coca-Cola sign above the door. The interior was dim and cluttered, with unvarnished wood floors and rickety storage shelves that were stacked to the ceiling with dusty boxes—Oxy and Lux, Ivory Flakes and Silver Snow, Rinso and Dreft and Purex. Against the back wall, next to a potbellied stove, was a big round table where the neighborhood regulars sat.

The regulars were old men mostly, drinkers and idlers. They earned their keep, or at least old Wehrle's grudging acquiescence, by running messages. Wehrle's had the only telephone for blocks around, and whenever a long-distance call came in, one of the regulars would dash out to fetch its recipient. My mother, Dorothy, remembers playing in the front yard one summer afternoon when a Wehrle's regular came up breathlessly with the news from Chicago that she now had a baby sister.

Chief among the regulars was a small, loud, relentlessly humorous man named Earnest C. Martindale. He had bristling brown hair, a thin face, a mouth that seemed eternally raised in a grin, and bright, birdlike eyes. He was a jokester, a tale teller, a spinner of rumor and innuendo. His mind was a bottomless well of groaners, wheezers, knee-slappers, and ribpokers. He was serious only for as long as it took to pass on some lurid new bit of gossip about a neighbor. Nobody ever thought the name Earnest suited him, so he was known as Marty.

Marty was from an Indiana farming family. He'd hated the farming life and had never gotten along with his father, so when he was a teenager he ran away from home. This was during the First World War; he lied about his age and enlisted in the navy. But he hated the navy, too, and confessed his lie in order to get discharged. The navy sent him home to his father. A few months later he ran away again and reenlisted; when he tried to get out again, his father told the navy to keep him. That was how he ended up as a grease monkey in the submarine corps.

At Wehrle's, he liked to tell horrible stories about his time in combat—though never when another veteran was in earshot. But whatever had happened to him during the war, his career in the navy ended up a success. He stayed on in the service after the armistice; he learned the rudiments of electrical engineering and rose to chief petty officer. Later, back in civilian life, he spent a couple of aimless years working odd jobs at factories around the Midwest before hiring on as an electrician at the Wood River refinery.

Now he lived in a rooming house off Troy Road and spent his mornings before work and his weekend afternoons hanging around Wehrle's. He liked Saturdays best, because that was when the women in the neighborhood dawdled over their shopping. He flirted with everyone. But on weekdays he reserved all his attention for Hilda.

Hilda came by every morning to buy a bag of fresh-baked sweet rolls for breakfast. She pretended to ignore Marty, and when she couldn't keep that up, she snorted in disgust at his risqué jokes. But each day she seemed to linger a little longer by the pastry counter.

Hilda was in her late twenties then. But she looked and she felt much older. She was worn out by her years of caring for Franciska and Agnes; her life was a perpetual trudge through chores and errands and favors and visits. Her only real diversion came in the summer, when her nieces and nephew visited from Chicago. She longed to have children and a house of her own—but since her wild years as a teenager, she'd almost never been alone in a man's company. So when Marty asked her to the movies she surprised herself by saying yes. Soon she started inviting him over for Sunday dinner after church.

Those dinners were still the high point of the household's week. But by then they were sparsely attended. Most of the neighborhood regulars had drifted away, missing Bosh's hospitality or Agnes's cooking. Because Hilda disapproved of alcohol, she'd given away all of Bosh's old wines—and while she laid out an enormous spread, her taste ran to the overboiled and undersalted. Now there were always staggering amounts of leftovers at the end of the meal, which Hilda would stash in their fancy new refrigerator, and for the rest of the week, the household would plow through beef stews and beef hashes and cold beef sandwiches on white bread.

Marty's arrival came as a shot in the arm. He always kept the table lively; soon some of the old crowd drifted back just to see what he'd say next. He was a real artist at needling, never happier than when he had the entire table laughing—except for his red-faced, furious target. One time he subjected ten-year-old Dorothy from Chicago to a feeble wheeze about pickles growing on a pickle tree, and for weeks afterward he'd nudge his dinner companions and point at her, saying, "Dorothy thinks pickles grow on trees." Telling me the story sixty years later, Dorothy got angry all over again.

It wasn't long before Hilda was the only one there who could stand him. Agnes was suspicious of him, Helen loathed him, and the other guests grew sick to death of him. But nobody ever dreamed of telling him he wasn't welcome.

Marty and Eugene detested each other from the beginning. Eugene broke his silence at the dinner table one afternoon by threatening, with no provocation anybody could detect, to punch Marty out. After that Marty grew cautious around Eugene. But he wasn't the sort of man who could forgo malice altogether. It just took him a while to find a way in.

The Wood River refinery, where both men worked, provided the opening. They were assigned to different shifts and rarely saw each other. But that didn't keep Marty from implying, and sometimes openly saying, that it was only through his influence with management that Eugene had been hired. It was a brilliant stroke. Eugene hated being beholden to anyone; the thought that people might believe he owed anything to Marty was almost too much for him to bear. At Sunday dinners from then on Eugene was so livid he could barely bring himself to look in Marty's direction. Whenever their eyes did meet, Marty would beam with satisfaction.

But then came the topper. Early in the spring of 1943 Marty showed up for Sunday dinner in a navy uniform. He announced to the table that he'd reenlisted. He was in his forties then, and he had been granted the same exemption from service that Eugene had—but he said he just couldn't sit idly by when his country needed him. So he'd joined the Seabees, the navy's new construction battalions, and he'd been recommissioned as a chief petty officer.

Everybody was impressed. Helen and Agnes grudgingly admitted he was a hero. The whole neighborhood came to his send-off, and before it was over, even Eugene had to shake his hand and wish him luck.

That was the last straw for Eugene. He enlisted the next day.

Eugene applied to the Seabees, and he was immediately accepted; by that point in the war, trained electricians, even electricians' helpers, were in desperately short supply. That spring he was on a train headed for a new Seabees base in

California. The train swarmed with fresh-faced soldiers, most nervous and some openly terrified. As they passed through the black, empty country west of the Mississippi, the car was filled with a ceaseless racket of anxious talk and panicky laughter. But none of that bothered Eugene. If there was one skill he'd mastered in life, it was how to sleep soundly on a loud moving train.

At the height of the war, travelers passing through Union Station in Chicago were greeted by a strange apparition. The great concourse was a perpetual hubbub of soldiers and sailors and marines jostling and queuing and laughing and hailing one another; huge lurid posters warned of eavesdropping spies (LOOK WHO'S LISTENING!); war bonds banners and a riot of flags representing all the Allied nations from India to Norway hung beneath the vast windows; and high up above it all, suspended in nets at the arched ceiling, were toy airplanes. There were thousands upon thousands of toy airplanes, arranged in countless close-packed rows and phalanxes; it was as though the contents of every toy box in Chicago had been drafted. They represented the government's goal of building a hundred thousand military planes a year.

To the three Sehnert kids, the sight was like a gateway into the war. Their own lives hadn't actually changed much since Pearl Harbor. Their father, Clarence, had a war-related exemption because of his job at the post office, and he'd felt no temptation to enlist. Mostly the kids were aware of the war as a series of shortages and disappearances, of men around the neighborhood departing unexpectedly, of cardboard stars popping up in windows like lanterns to announce that someone in the house had gone into the service. One year there was no chewing gum; it was because of the war, they were told—so the kids chewed the softened tar that bubbled off the streets on hot days. And there was never enough gasoline for the car—which was why, when it came time to go to Edwardsville each summer, they now traveled grandly by train.

On their way through downstate Illinois they saw a countryside alive with the war. There were frequent unscheduled stops in small towns to take on waves of uniformed passengers; then there'd be interminable waits on meadowy sidings so that trains with a higher priority could roar past. Everywhere the idle factories and mines and mills were beehives of new life. The Hoovervilles had all emptied out, and the homeless had come in off the road to work—so many that there was nowhere to put them. In towns all through the heartland, tent cities were set up to house the overflow workers; people called them New Hoovervilles.

Edwardsville was consumed by war fever. All the storefront windows downtown were red-white-and-blue explosions of flags and bunting. All the derelict factories were running full shifts—the Nelson foundry was reopened to make artillery shells. There were new parades and drives every week: rubber drives, tin drives, brass drives, paper drives, blood drives, even drives to collect used cooking fat (to manufacture glycerin). At the climax of one scrap metal drive, the veterans of the Great War towed the cannon in front of the American Legion hall across town to the collection point at the dump. Another time, a traveling military show arrived bearing a great prize: a Japanese miniature submarine; it was paraded around the streets like a captured dragon. In the city park, beneath a stand of gigantic elms, a big flag-festooned sign went up that listed every local man and woman in the service. Helen sometimes took the kids there so they could admire Eugene's name.

Even the house on Second Avenue had the feel of a military outpost. Helen hung an enormous map of the world in the dining room, and each morning after breakfast, she'd go through the newspapers and then ceremoniously push in pins to mark the sites of Allied victories. She also insisted, to Agnes's horror, on listening to the radio during dinner; she would shush everyone so they could hear the latest bulletins from the front. The kids were immediately drafted. They helped tend the victory gardens on Second Avenue, and on the weekends they rolled bandages at the Red Cross. But their main job was to answer the letters from Eugene.

Nobody had really expected to hear from Eugene at all. But he wrote constantly. The letters bunched up in transit; the postman would sometimes, with a sort of mock disapproval, present Agnes with a wad of five or ten letters rubberbanded together. The letters quickly exhausted Agnes's ability to respond, and Helen ran out of things to say even faster than that. So the task was turned over to the kids.

Mainly Eugene wrote to ask how things were back home. He inquired constantly about the family and the household, particularly his dogs. The kids wrote back that everybody was fine and that the dogs were doing well; they didn't tell him that in fact Helen was spoiling the dogs outrageously.

Eugene also wrote about what he was doing. But he seemed to assume they knew all about it already; they couldn't make any sense out of his talk of dredges and generators and landing strips. All they got was that he was doing something big on an island in the South Pacific. Sometimes he recorded progress toward cryptic goals: *Well today we layed cable down to the gas farm. Well it was hotter than anything but we got the juice going.* Only once or twice did he say anything at all about what he was feeling: *Its awful lonesome here but like they say we got to get the job done.* Sometimes he made vague references to his fellow soldiers. *There are a lot of funny guys here. Ones from San Fran and ones from De Moines and ones from New York.* That was all he said about them; it was as though he thought that a guy being from anywhere other than Edwardsville was in itself funny.

One other person was missing from the household in those days: Hilda. But she never wrote and she was never discussed.

When the kids arrived in the summer of 1943, she was simply gone, and nobody would say where she went. Agnes bristled whenever she was mentioned, and Helen looked despondent.

Gradually the kids gathered that Hilda was in Virginia. She was working at a shirt factory near the big navy base on the coast. They vaguely assumed it was some special war-related job. But one evening when they were sitting on the front porch, Helen lost interest in their game of movie stars and at last told them the truth: Hilda had gone to Virginia to be with Marty.

That was how the children and the rest of the family learned that Hilda and Marty had gotten married.

Eugene's first sight of Bougainville was as the convoy approached from the west. The island was a low line of mist-shrouded greenery rising up to a broken mountain range. Along the range were two active volcanoes. For all the time Eugene was there, the volcanoes never stopped belching vast billows of brilliant white smoke.

The Seabees were put ashore on a narrow strip of sand between the ocean and a brackish swamp. The interior of the swamp was an impassable tangle swarming with mysterious life: there were rainbow-brilliant birds swooping in and out of the dense tree canopy, and poisonous snakes slithering through stagnant pools, and swarms of unnamed insects rising in waves of red mist to bite like fire. The underbrush was so thick that when a plane went down a hundred yards from the beach, it took the search teams five days to find the wreckage.

For weeks, the Seabees pounded their way inward. They dug canals and dammed the streams; they dynamited the trees; they poured dirt and rocks and tree trunks into the stagnant ponds and bulldozed them over. It was miserable work. Every afternoon, torrential rains fell, and the nights were bone-chillingly cold. But in a month the crews had cleared and graded enough land to lay down the metal netting of an airstrip. Two weeks later, a crippled fighter used the strip for an emergency landing. That night the camp held a riotous party. Eugene wrote home that it was the proudest moment of his life.

The weather broke soon afterward, and work on the base accelerated. By New Year's Day of 1944, there were two functioning airstrips; one of them was for heavy bombers and it was more than a mile long. Roads had been cut all around the airfield to the docks, and the bay was being dredged for a permanent harbor. The tanks of the fuel farm held ten thousand gallons apiece, with pumps running to the hangars. Rivers diverted from the interior brought fresh drinking water. And in the original jungle clearing there now stood barracks, a mess hall, officers' and enlisted men's clubs, and a movie theater.

Up until then Eugene had paid almost no attention to the Japanese. Everybody knew they were on the island. They had an air base on the other side of the mountains. Every few days, one of their planes would buzz the American camp like a stray horsefly. But otherwise they were invisible. (After the war it was learned that the Japanese had ignored the American presence on the island for months because they didn't think anybody could survive in the swamps.) This didn't change until sometime after New Year's, when Eugene was roped into a crew delivering supplies to the patrols on the perimeter.

It was trackless country, out beyond the last Seabee road. The trucks got mired in the mud; Eugene and the rest of the crew had to lug the rations and water barrels on their backs. The patrols they were resupplying were dug into the foothills of the mountain range. Everyone suspected that there were Japanese soldiers somewhere above. But the weather had turned foul, and fog shrouded the jungle; nothing could be seen up the slopes but weird dim silhouettes melting into gray. Just as Eugene's crew got ready to head back to the base, there was a noise they'd never heard before. It was a rattle like the first stirrings of an avalanche. Men started yelling in panic. Bounding down the slopes out of the fog was a cascade of live grenades.

After that the Americans were perpetually on edge. But the big battle didn't come till weeks later. An immense Japanese force slowly crossed the mountains and surreptitiously surrounded the American base. Eugene spent the night before the expected attack in a foxhole behind one of the airstrips. The forward patrols swept the line of the jungle with searchlights; nobody could see anything other than a frenzy of darting shadows. The night was humid and close. Thick clouds were hanging down almost low enough to touch. Toward morning somebody had the idea of turning up the searchlights. The trick worked. The glare coming off the underbelly of the cloud deck illuminated the depths of the jungle and revealed the Japanese artillery positions. Then the firefight began. Eugene wrote home that his foxhole was so well constructed all the other guys wanted to hide in it.

Then he didn't write for months. The next anybody heard from him was late in the spring of 1944. He'd left Bougainville; his battalion had been rotated behind the line, but he'd been transferred to another battalion and was now in the Marshall Islands. That was all he said. The next letter came in the middle of summer; he wrote to say that he had been transferred again and was now on the island of Saipan. There were no more letters from him after that.

The war ended the next year. Over that summer and fall, Edwardsville's veterans came swarming home. Among them were Hilda and Marty. They arrived at Second Avenue together and immediately moved into Eugene's old attic room. There seemed to be no good reason to refuse them. Nobody had heard from Eugene in more than a year—and besides, Hilda explained, it was only temporary, until they found a house of their own.

At the end of 1945, Agnes got an official letter informing her that Eugene was in a navy hospital in Australia. The following spring, another official notification arrived: Eugene had been transferred stateside to a hospital in California near Yosemite. He was suffering from war-related mental illness. He was not allowed visitors and was unable to answer letters.

Agnes told the family he had malaria.

8

Nobody Would Ever Guess

THE FRONT ROOM of Clarence and Mary's apartment in Ravenswood was always gloomy. But during the late 1940s, it did have one bright spot of color: *Arizona Highways* magazine. This was a slick publication with a lot of arty photographs of Southwestern landscapes. Mary's widowed mother in Tucson had given them a gift subscription. Mary herself didn't like it much, and Clarence never read it (or anything else); it was on display only to impress guests.

But it did have one faithful reader in the house: their oldest daughter, Dorothy. She would sneak into the parlor on lonely afternoons and flip through the issues that were fanned out on the parlor table. She'd never been out of Illinois, and she was spellbound by the mysterious images of the Petrified Forest and Sunset Crater and the Painted Desert. They seemed as remote and alluring as the moons of Mars.

Dorothy was a shy and unadventurous girl. She was painfully unassertive, easily intimidated, a backbencher in school, a wallflower at dances, ignored by salesclerks and waitresses. She once told me that the most mortifying moment of her life came when she was nine years old, at a movie theater on Irving Park Boulevard, during a showing of *The Wizard of Oz*. It was when the Wicked Witch wrote *SURRENDER DOROTHY* on the skies above the Emerald City.

But she also had a secret hunger to get out into the larger world. In 1948 she became the first person in the family since Clarence to graduate high school. She next spent two years at a community college and another year working as a secretary in an office to earn tuition money. Then she made her move. She amazed and impressed her parents with the announcement that she wanted to go to Arizona and attend Arizona State University.

When Eugene at last came back to Edwardsville, everybody made a point of telling him how good he looked. They'd all heard he'd been in the hospital with malaria—and everybody knew that malaria took a lot out of you. You could tell just by looking at Eugene. He had always been thin and quiet; now he was gaunt, fidgety, sunken cheeked, and practically mute.

But he said nothing whatever about malaria, or about anything else that might have happened to him. If anybody asked him anything about the war, he stalked out of the room.

Nor did he make any comment about what he found at home, about how Hilda had married his old nemesis, Marty, nor even about how the two of them had taken over his attic refuge. Instead he immediately set to work on a home-improvement project. He walled off part of the kitchen to make a new bedroom for himself, and he installed a heavy door that he could lock from the inside.

He returned to work at the refinery. His old job had been guaranteed to him as a veteran—but the company probably would have hired him anyway, no matter how shaky he looked. The end of the war hadn't reduced the demand for petroleum and petroleum-derived products, as had been expected. Instead sales were accelerating almost exponentially. The refinery had full crews around the clock. It had undergone one major expansion since the war and was already so far beyond design capacity that they were planning the next. They needed every warm body they could find, and Eugene fit the bill.

He volunteered for any task that kept him away from people. His main job was routine maintenance—checking the hundreds of miles of overburdened wiring woven around the refinery grounds. He was happy to work the graveyard shift. Hour after hour, he'd drive a company pickup truck down the cinder roads along the outer fences. He'd stop and tweak and fiddle with the countless generators and relays and circuit breakers. He'd go out to the complex of pumps by the main highway, where the tanker trucks were lined up, then to the station by the levee, where the barges were gathered on the floodlit river, and at last he went to survey the new radio-controlled pipeline system that was sending a ceaseless river of refined oil out east toward the Ohio River valley.

In the dead hours after midnight he did a slow sweep through the tank farm. This was where the oceans of crude oil coming in from the fields of Kansas and Oklahoma and Texas were stored. The immense round tanks were laid out in neat rows like a new suburban subdivision. Usually Eugene was the only human being on its streets. The floodlights on the tanks cast absurdly elongated shadows around him as he walked. In the distance, the main refinery complex stood up against the fumes of the night sky in a bristling, jeweled confusion. There was no sound but remote mechanical hoots and wails and, in summer, the shriek of cicadas in the weeds.

At home he retreated into a deeper solitude. He gave up on his old passion for hunting—his companions August and Frank had died, and besides, after the war he couldn't bear to hold a gun any longer. (He still kept hunting dogs, though, and he built them elaborate doghouses in the backyard.) He rarely left the house. He hated movies, he refused to eat at restaurants, and he never showed the slightest interest in seeing women socially. He couldn't even be coaxed into going down the block to a neighbor's house for dinner. "We've got plenty of food at home," he'd say.

His main enthusiasm was gardening. He'd taken it up in the hospital at the advice of one of his doctors—the last few months there, he'd passed the time by tending the flower beds along the hospital walkways and around the parking lot. Once he got home, he started reading seed catalogs and ordering all manner of exotic bulbs. Each year he appropriated more and more of the backyard. Gradually he built up a fantastical labyrinth of flower beds and stakes and trellises that only he could follow. Day after day, even in the hottest weather, he withdrew into its sunlit depths, where he worked for hours in absolute silence.

He became something of a legend around that part of Edwardsville—the gaunt old recluse with his mysterious comings and goings, who never had a word to say. "After he got out of the hospital," Dorothy says, "he never talked to any of us again." But one of his neighbors told me a story. She happened to have been standing near the back fence of her house on a summer evening as a freight train trundled past. A figure jumped down from the caboose and sauntered along the alley. It wasn't until the figure passed her by that she recognized who it was: Eugene. He smiled, held a finger to his lips, and then turned in through the back gate of the Sehnert house and vanished into his gardens.

Dorothy left Chicago for Arizona at the end of the summer of 1951. Her parents paid for an airline ticket. It was the first time she had ever flown. By the time the plane landed, she was already in love with the Southwestern landscape. A few weeks after her arrival in Tempe, she was happier than she'd ever been in her life. ASU had a reputation even then as a party school, and it wasn't long before Dorothy had joined a sorority, dyed her hair blond, and started going to dances.

One autumn evening during her second year at school, she and her sorority sisters went to a chaperoned dance at the local air force base. The base was in the desert outside of town. It was an immense military city that had been built during World War II and had recently been reactivated to train pilots for Korea. The sorority girls arrived to find that a new rec hall had been spiffed up for them. Long folding tables with white tablecloths bore phalanxes of diminutive Coke bottles, each with its own carefully bent paper straw. Towering vases of gladioli stood in the corners of the hall like sentries. The band wore dress uniforms and played bland, genial swing, while a girl in a dazzling white frock stood at the microphone and did her best Rosemary Clooney.

The cadets were buffed, scrubbed, and excruciatingly polite. They danced with decorous precision; they held the girls firmly by the hand and pressed gently at the small of the back as though carrying a fragile statue. Midway through the evening, Dorothy was approached by a cadet who said he was asking for a dance on behalf of somebody else—this way, he explained, she could refuse without embarrassment to either party. She wanted to know who was really asking, and he pointed out a cadet on the other side of the room. The cadet was short and muscular, with a broad pug face, crew-cut black hair, and (as it shortly proved) a courtly manner and an Okie drawl. This was Henry Lee Sandlin.

He was charming. He was witty. He was elaborately solicitous of her opinions. He talked casually and dismissively about his own hardscrabble life: his childhood in the dust bowl as one of eight children raised by a widowed mother, his escape from a small town via a scholarship to a state university and enlistment in the air force. He'd always loved flying, he told her, but immediately added that he had no intention of being a professional pilot; once he was back from Korea he was going to strike out on his own to make his fortune.

Dorothy had never met anybody like him in her life. She thought he looked and acted just like the glamorous World War II fighter ace Philip Cochran, who had flown daring combat missions in North Africa and Burma. (Cochran had grown so famous from magazine stories and newsreels that an instantly recognizable caricature, "Flip Corkin," showed up as a hero in the comic strip *Terry and the Pirates*.) As they danced, she remembers, "I became completely smitten."

During a lull in the dancing they went outside. It was a luminous evening. The sky was a wash of brilliant coral, the hills were lavender, and the towers and hangars of the base were india ink. There were constellations of pink and white and blue lights glittering on the airfields. Henry told Dorothy that he'd worked on a ranch when he was a teenager; he said teasingly that she probably never thought she'd dance with a cowboy. She replied that she thought cowboys were roughhousers with no manners. Not true, he answered: What about Roy Rogers and Gene Autry? And then, in a sweet tenor, he began crooning "Happy Trails to You."

That was how my parents met.

In Edwardsville, old Agnes had her life arranged almost exactly the way she wanted it. Essentially nothing about the house had changed since Bosh had left her a widow more than twenty years before. The overstuffed armchairs and blackened-mahogany headboards, the sun-faded floral wallpaper and fossilized lace doilies—they were all just as they'd been in Bosh's time. She still sat each day in her rocking chair in the bay window. Eugene had planted African violets right outside, and their tendrils wound around the windowframe like an illuminated border. Sometimes she laughed or sang to herself. Other times she carried on long conversations with someone unseen. When people heard her, they'd say, "She's talking to Bosh."

She thought about her children the way she always did: that is, she was unyieldingly fierce toward her daughters and adoring toward her sons. She doted on Eugene and refused to admit there was anything odd about him. She was just as indulgent toward her oldest son, Clarence, who visited once a year from Chicago. Clarence had grown to be foolish and disrespectful about the family house; he found it unfailingly hilarious how primitive everything was. One time he brought a gift for the outhouse: an ornate sign he'd carved in his work-room that read *Johnny's Place*. Agnes hated it, as she hated all indecent jokes—but in deference to her son's sense of humor, she insisted on nailing it to the outhouse door, and it stayed there for years.

The big thorn in her side was her son-in-law Marty. He and Hilda still made no sign of moving out into a place of their own. Marty was bringing home a steady paycheck from the refinery, but he paid no rent and kicked in for the daily expenses only at rare intervals and with a great show of reluc-tant magnanimity. His main contribution to the household was a set of flatware he said he'd stolen during the war from an admiral's mess. It was made of steel and was stamped *USN*.

Marty never did any chores. He said that was women's work, and besides, he was getting too old and creaky. He expected Hilda, Helen, and Agnes to wait on him—though only Hilda obliged. He installed himself in one of the easy chairs in the parlor, despite the intense disapproval of Helen; she thought the parlor should be reserved for guests. But Agnes tolerated his presence there. She took it as a tacit admission that he really was a guest and not a permanent resident—and besides, it served as a quarantine for his cheap, foul cigars.

During Agnes's last years, she found another nemesis: the new minister at her church. She'd loved the old hotheaded minister; his replacement was a drooping, soft-spoken, and perpetually troubled young man who condemned no one and kept hinting that his flock should examine the society of Edwardsville for signs of creeping social injustice. Agnes had never heard such nonsense. Desperate for that old hellfire, she began reading the Bible for herself. She was particularly drawn to Revelation. As she balefully regarded Marty's comings and goings, she found it soothing to talk about the skies peeling back to reveal the fury of the Lamb on the Lord's day, when all the secrets of the human heart would stand revealed.

Clarence still worked at Chicago's municipal airport. After the war it was renamed Midway, after the famous naval victory. By the early 1950s, it was the busiest airport in the world, and "Midway" had become a global byword for confusion, over-crowding, and misdirection. The mail room had swelled into a spilling empire of overwork; Clarence was exhausted and frazzled at the end of each shift. He longed for retirement, and he dreamed of selling his house and going out on the road with Mary. Then, too, he'd recently developed a racking cough—which he blamed not on his cigarette smoking but on Midway's new kind of smog: the exhaust from jet airplanes.

Agnes died in the spring of 1954. She was the first of the Sehnerts to die in a hospital and the last to be buried in Edwardsville's ancient, crowded Catholic cemetery. There was just room for her beside Bosh, amid the jostle of beseeching angels and grinning cherubs.

Once Agnes was gone, her children tore up the house. They walled off a corner of the kitchen next to Eugene's room and had a proper bathroom built, with a toilet, a sink, and a shower. They installed faucets with running water in the kitchen sink. They had trenches dug across the front yard to connect the plumbing to the water supply and the sewer system. They put a phone on the kitchen wall and another in the dining room. They replaced the coal furnace with a gas furnace. They knocked down the outhouse and put up a garage. They brought home a television set and put it beside the enormous old radio in the parlor; in the evenings they watched it through the doorway as they sat at the dining room table.

Helen finally unbent a little. She rid the master bedroom of Agnes's possessions and took the big old bed entirely for herself. She brought home her movie magazines and displayed them brazenly on the dining room sideboard. She had her hair done at a beauty parlor downtown. She began taking vacations away from home. Sometimes she traveled with a church group; other times she went on bus tours with her friend Irene, who lived across the train tracks on First Avenue. And at the age of forty-four, she took driving lessons and bought herself a car.

Edwardsville's first shopping center was built south of town, on Troy Road just past Second Avenue. It was a hulk of gleaming white concrete set within an immense lagoon of asphalt. There was a shoe store, a haberdashery, an appliance store, and a store that sold ladies' handbags. The anchor store was a supermarket. It was an enormous place. It had wide aisles, long rows of freezers, and floors of gleaming black-and-white linoleum; it sold TV dinners and frozen cinnamon rolls, cake mixes and Cheez Whiz; the baked goods were all brand names, and the butcher counter sealed all the meats in plastic; there were automatic doors that magically puffed open when you approached them, and there was Muzak playing over the loudspeakers. Nobody in town had ever seen anything like it. It immediately drove the corner groceries in the neighborhood out of business.

By the corral of shopping carts near the main entrance were a couple of stone benches. That's where the regulars from Wehrle's grocery made their new home on weekend afternoons. They continued their old round of gossip and banter about everybody who came in and out of the automatic doors. Marty appointed himself the supermarket's concierge. Whenever the doors burst open and a woman emerged, he'd immediately hop up and offer to carry her bags. As he bustled with her out into the parking lot he'd pay courtly compliments, or tell off-color jokes, or hint at lurid gossip about a neighbor—anything that might provoke a blush and an unstated invitation to continue. Then, as he paused before the open car trunk, grocery bags dangling precariously, he'd make a cryptic reference to his own sad situation. If he got the slightest encouragement, he'd launch into the story.

That was how the whole town learned about his unhappy marriage.

According to Marty it was simple: Hilda had been all gung ho to get married—but it turned out she didn't like sex. So what was he to do? He was a normal man with normal needs. Didn't anybody appreciate what kind of strength it took to continue on in this impossible situation? He declared that there were times when he wanted to walk down the train tracks into the woods and blow his brains out.

He repeated his story, in one version or another, to almost every woman he met. Eventually, one rainy Saturday afternoon when he was stuck at home, he told it to Helen. They were alone in the house at the time. After he got to the part about suicide, he grabbed her and tried to kiss her. She slapped him and struggled free. He laughed as though it were just a joke. He sank back into his easy chair while she stormed out of the house.

Helen was left so enraged that a few days later she broke down and talked to Hilda about it. Or she tried to. Almost as soon as she started, Hilda cut her off and said she didn't need to hear any more. She already knew what Marty was like.

Clarence retired from the post office once his youngest daughter, Nancy, got married. Soon afterward he sold the old brownstone three-flat in Ravenswood and bought a sleek silvery Airstream trailer. It was twenty-six feet long; it had a built-in shower and toilet, a kitchen with an electric stove and broiler, a bed, a foldout dinette table, a butane water heater, a septic tank, and closets and cabinets with special imported "Sta-Closed" closet catches. He hitched it to the back of his new wood-paneled station wagon, and then he and Mary were ready to go.

They had nowhere in mind for a destination, and they were in no hurry to arrive. At first they stayed mostly at campgrounds and national parks. Clarence always had a comfortable routine there. He got up each day before sunrise and set out on his own, to hike or hunt or fish in perfect solitude. He rarely came back before sunset. Mary was left behind at the trailer. She soon grew restless and bored. She'd never had any use for the outdoors in the first place; she'd only ever put up with it as a way of being alone with Clarence. Her idea of perfect relaxation had been to spend afternoons with her friends in Ravenswood, playing pinochle and canasta and listening to their favorite crooners on the radio. So, as an act of self-preservation, she eventually persuaded Clarence to start staying in trailer parks.

There were trailer parks scattered all over the country by then. Some were rudimentary places where the occupants turned over almost as fast as they would at a drive-in movie. Others were much more ornate. They found one outside of Tucson that had street signs at the intersections, gardens planted around the larger plots, and its own little downtown, a general store and a Laundromat and a communal shower next to the manager's office. Mary liked it there; she made friends, and she could always find a card game or an impromptu party going on in the afternoons. Clarence liked being able to go off by himself on extended fishing trips in the mountains. They ended up staying there more than a year.

Mary was fascinated by her neighbors. In the next plot was an older couple in a big hulking mobile home that looked wholly immovable. The husband was a retired bank president; the wife used to belong to a country club. They always wore Hawaiian shirts and shorts, and they gave parties that they called luaus, where they passed out leis and tropical drinks and played *South Pacific* on their hi-fi. Next to them was a jovial young corporate executive; he called his squat slab of a trailer "the canned ham," and he was staying in it only because his company was constantly transferring him from branch office to branch office and he didn't think he'd last out the lease on an apartment. Across the way was a shy young Bohemian couple from Albuquerque who had set out to see the country with a battered teardrop trailer and had made it only as far as Arizona. At the corner lived a woman Mary's age who was an artist; she did paintings of cacti and fence posts against lurid desert sunsets. She was another Airstream owner; she wore turquoise-bead necklaces and fringed vests, she listened to Van Cliburn records, and once she shocked and impressed Mary by serving her a mimosa at breakfast.

Clarence was indifferent to them all. But he did sometimes allow Mary to coax him over to one neighboring trailer or another for an evening card game. He was bored by bridge, but he did like poker—even though they were only penny-ante games, and he was never as good at it as Mary got to be. So he would grudgingly sit with everyone else at the card tables set up under the trailer canopy. He might even now and then unbend enough to join in when they argued about the menace of *Sputnik* or the hot-rodders on the desert roads outside of town.

But then one spring night Clarence and Mary were coming back home after a particularly good evening of poker. They were strolling along one of the dirt paths outlined in bottle glass along the edge of the trailer park. There was a full moon; a breeze sprang up, and brought out of the desert the smell of sage. Mary suddenly became aware of how restless and irritable Clarence had been lately. She abruptly announced that she was sick of the trailer park and it was time to get back on the road.

Mary found a new hobby. She took up painting. She went about it with her usual practicality. She bought how-to books and read them all from cover to cover. She stocked up on art supplies whenever they passed through a large town. Wherever they camped, she'd get out her easel and busy herself with small, rigorously proportioned landscape studies. At first she painted mountains and forests—views with simple and stark forms. Then she grew more confident and began painting whatever she saw along the road as they traveled.

Over the years, she painted old railcar diners and desert bus stations, derelict farmhouses and antique gas stations, flower-draped stone fountains and thickets of masts in harbors. There were dozens of paintings of the Florida Keys, where she and Clarence often spent their winters; they would find an isolated islet along the chain, park on a deserted beach, and spend weeks at a time there unobserved. There were even more paintings of Door County in Wisconsin. They had a particular secluded cove where they liked to spend their summers. Mary painted the cottages along the shore, and the little maze of docks where the fishing boats swayed, and the shabby tavern decorated with old boating gear and car tires that was the only commercial building for miles around.

She didn't care what happened to her paintings at first. She gave them away to family and friends, and to anybody who complimented them. But then she got the idea to sell them. People wanted them for souvenirs; they liked these little glimpses of the older America that was vanishing off to the sides of the new interstates. So wherever they stopped from then on, at a tourist attraction or at a new trailer park, she'd set up a display of her paintings next to the Airstream, and she always did a brisk business.

One October in the early 1960s, Helen drove out from Edwardsville to New Mexico. That was the longest trip she ever took on her own. She had been planning to go on another bus tour with her friend Irene, but at the last minute, Irene had come down with the flu. Helen couldn't change her vacation time, so she decided to spend the two weeks camping out in the desert with Clarence and Mary. Mary found her to be a good companion. She had no interest whatever in nature and she didn't need to be entertained. After Clarence went tromping off each morning, the two women would pass the whole day together at the trailer, Mary painting and Helen contentedly reading her magazines.

Helen did get on Mary's nerves eventually. She spent way too much time complaining. Her chief complaint was about Marty's presence in the Edwardsville house. She was still livid about the time he tried to kiss her. But whenever she tired of that subject, she proved to have an inexhaustible storehouse of earlier grievances to draw upon. One time she was in a confiding mood and told Mary a secret from her past: the story about her brief flirtation before the war and about the oath she'd sworn to Agnes never to marry.

If she'd been looking for sympathy, she'd picked the wrong person. Mary was incredulous. She briskly told Helen to find some good, steady, reliable, dull man to settle down with—and pronto.

That made Helen laugh. There were no men for her, she said. If there ever had been any, they'd died in the war, and now she was too old. But then she got a sly, secretive look on her face. She said there was someone she liked—but that was her business, and nobody would ever guess who it was.

9

One Last Parade

BY THE MID-1960S, a new generation of Sehnert children, Clarence and Mary's grandchildren, had begun coming to Edwardsville in the summers. We were folded into the household as though it had been ready for us all our lives; we were immediately immersed in those rules and customs and family traditions that we were supposed to absorb and master without a word.

One rule in particular I detested. Every day, I had to take a nap. I never understood why—some atavistic idea about proper childhood development, maybe. It always happened when the afternoon was at its hottest. Hilda would order me to lie down on the huge old bed in the master bedroom, and there I'd have to stay for an hour, pretending to sleep and trying not to suffocate.

The room was dim and sweltering. The furniture was a

mountain range of gloom. The bedding smelled of laundry soap and musty flowers. I would look idly around the room and study the pastel water stains on the wallpaper; the stains always reminded me of the islands on treasure maps, and I would let my gaze wander all over them, plotting out pirate expeditions and desperate voyages of escape. Sometimes a ray of sun escaped from the blind and I'd watch it creep across the quilt and stir up a little turmoil of dust motes in its wake. Then I would think about the way light was moving around the house—the honeyed light in the attic bedroom, which on the hottest days was like a golden furnace; the dusty pewter light in the basement pantry, falling on the rows of preserves in jars and making them glow in brilliant pastels.

Then I'd count up everything I hated about staying at the house. There was no air-conditioning. No record player. No books. Nothing to do and nothing to think about. There was a TV in the parlor, but we weren't permitted to turn it on. There was also a magnificent old radio in a carved wooden case, its rows of Bakelite switches and buttons suggesting a Buck Rogers spaceship; we could play with that all we liked. The dials would light up, but it wouldn't produce any sound.

Then I would listen for sounds of life elsewhere. At long intervals a crackling noise would come from the parlor: that was Marty taking the cellophane off a cigar. Or else there'd be a bang in the kitchen: Hilda shutting a cabinet door. Hilda and Marty seemed to have no problem being around each other without speaking a word. Sometimes, if Helen was home from work, I'd hear her shuffling and snapping cards at the dining room table. Once in a while there'd be a faint sound from the window: the squeak of a faucet or the distant rumble of a wheelbarrow. That was Eugene laboring away in the gardens.

Occasionally I would find myself attentive to more elusive noises: the sighs and groans of ancient floorboards, the rustle of brittle lace curtains, the solemn tick of a clock, a fly buzzing at a screen window for admittance, a creak or thunk in an empty room. Sometimes I'd wonder whether anybody had died here. Then I'd stare up at the looming headboard and wonder whether it was about to fall and kill me. Then I'd start to believe I was already dead and was just waiting for the funeral procession to arrive.

Nobody in the house ever actually talked about the past. Their rules and lessons were presented as complete and beyond history, as neutral facts that had always been true. I thought of the house's inhabitants in the same way: they were as unchanging and immovable as Mount Rushmore. I assumed the four of them had always been in the house and that it had always belonged to them; their lives and personalities had become impossibly intertangled with it, as though in a root cellar.

Hilda went with the kitchen. That was the only cheerful room in the house. It had bright yellow walls and white counters, and in the summer there were always bowls of ripening peaches on the table and windowsill. The big appliances were prehistoric—but Hilda had recently allowed a few incursions of modernity: there was a gleaming four-slice toaster on the counter, and next to it was a Mixmaster that whirred like an outboard motor. She'd also started buying supermarket mainstays like Fluffo and Rice Krispies and Reddi-wip, and she'd sometimes make the strange recipes on the backs of the boxes. For the Fourth of July she'd concoct a huge quivering mold, with red and blue layers of Jell-O alternating with white layers of Jell-O and milk, and marshmallow blobs for stars.

Through the kitchen door was the dining room, and that belonged to Helen. She was invariably at the big oak table dealing out cards. She played solitaire and patience if there was no one around, and she taught the kids countless variations of Go Fish and Spit in the Ocean. But she was just as fascinated by the board games we brought with us from home, Clue and Risk and Candy Land and the Game of Life. She even learned to play a ridiculous James Bond Thunderball board game I had, in which teams of scuba-geared assassins engaged one another in an enfeebled version of Chinese checkers. No matter what we played, she was the fiercest competitor I'd ever seen. But I never saw her gloat; whenever she won, which was most of the time, she'd get no more than a crooked, secretive little smile, as though this was only what she deserved.

Across the hall was the parlor, which was Marty's domain. He'd retired from the refinery by then, and he spent each day from sunup to sunset sitting in his easy chair, smoking cigars and scattering newspapers around his feet. Sometimes he made a supreme effort and shuffled into the kitchen, where with a great groan he'd bend to fetch a snack out of the icebox. He complained unrelentingly about his aching back and his weary joints, and he routinely begged off doing chores or favors. He would shrug elaborately if anybody asked him a question about anything at all. "I just work here," he'd say.

I always wondered what work Marty did. He didn't go with the family to church; he never played cards with us after dinner; and when everybody was gathered out in the backyard in the late afternoons, he'd stay inside in the parlor. Day in and day out he wore pin-striped overalls and a train engineer's cap that was greasy with age. When I was little I thought he wore this outfit because he actually was an engineer, which to me was the finest job in the world, and I once made the mistake of telling him so. He looked at me in amazement; then he began bellowing with laughter. For days afterward he would point his finger at me and start laughing all over again.

I never liked him and tried to avoid him. He liked grabbing you if you strayed too close. He'd squeeze you by your shoulders and stare into your face, his eyes bright with a kind of avian malice. He would tell his jokes, a collection of wheezes weaker than Bazooka Joe; when you failed to laugh, he would look disapproving and poke your ribs, sometimes hard enough to leave a bruise. If you got upset, he would shake with laughter. For the rest of the day he'd announce to anybody within earshot that he'd discovered a secret crybaby.

Eugene was barely there. He still worked the midnight shift at the refinery, and if he was home he was usually hidden behind the locked door of his bedroom or holed up somewhere deep within the maze of his garden. At family gatherings he'd appear briefly, as though in silent protest, keeping in the background, saying nothing, looking at no one. He hated having his photograph taken; the only time I ever saw him get angry, or for that matter display emotion of any kind, was when he saw a cousin of mine pointing a camera at him. I found his remoteness fascinating, and I kept hoping he'd acknowledge me somehow. But the most I got out of him was a curious, barely perceptible nod of his head, and maybe a sort of smile (which I liked to think was one of secret complicity) before he vanished back behind the door of his bedroom, where I wasn't permitted to follow.

One time, though, when I was very young, he did speak to me—or maybe I just dreamed that he spoke to me. What I remember is this: I came around the corner of the house and found Eugene digging a deep ditch. There was someone with him, a man I didn't recognize, who was wearing an antique suit even though the day was punishingly hot. I asked what they were doing. Eugene said, "I'm digging a grave for my father."

I ran away. I found Helen in the dining room and stammered out what had just happened. She snorted in contempt. She said, "Eugene has a strange sense of humor."

By then, Eugene's gardens covered most of the property. The only open ground left was a swath of grass by the back fence, surrounding the immense old shade trees. There were green Adirondack chairs scattered beneath the trees like islets in the tide, and there was almost always a forgotten glass of lemonade sitting on an armrest, beaded with silver sweat.

Out the back fence was the alley where the train tracks ran. It was a hushed and sunny place. Nobody was ever around, and nothing ever moved; it had been years since the last train had come through. The tracks were wholly swallowed up by groves of towering weeds. A couple hundred yards down from the house were two derelict flatcars on a siding. They were floating on a bed of weeds as dense as the Sargasso Sea—which made them the ideal setting for pirate battles. One afternoon I drafted my cousins and some neighbor kids, and we staged an apocalyptic showdown there between Captain Nemo and Long John Silver, complicated by attacks from Godzilla, the Creature from the Black Lagoon, and a kid who claimed to be a giant octopus. I thought it was the high point of my life.

Other times I wandered along the tracks by myself. I kept my head down; I was searching for buried treasure. My mother had told me that when she was a kid she'd find odd little fish-shaped pebbles there that Hilda and Helen had claimed were Indian arrowheads. I never saw anything like that; my quest was for bottle caps. I got to be expert at spotting their peculiar trace. It was a little serrated line in the dirt, like the fin of a baby dinosaur. I'd pry one up and wipe away the clots of earth and stone to reveal an ancient cap. It would gleam with carnival-pinstripe red, white, and blue, or regal bronze and purple, or mysterious silver-black, for some soft drink flavor I could barely imagine: ginger wine, birch beer, blackberry cream.

I kept meandering on. The tracks led out past the edge of town, into a whole hushed world of tumbledown fences and shabby gardens, of overgrown pathways smelling of wildflowers and mint, of broken-windowed sheds engulfed by weeds. The afternoons were sultry and still; insects clicked and moaned in the underbrush. Grape-purple thunderclouds were building up in the west, somewhere beyond the Mississippi. Sometimes a wind would spring up ahead of a storm, and the meadow grasses would seethe, and a tree on a high hill would bend and quiver in a private ecstasy. I liked to imagine trains passing the way they had in the old days, and people posing in the observation cars as though in magazine ads, opening up their exotic soft drinks and flinging the caps off into the golden afternoon light.

Then the train tracks were gone. One spring the local power company got an easement and ripped them all out. When I arrived that summer, I found in their place a line of slim white power pylons taller than the highest trees. The track bed had been bulldozed flat and a ragged strip of blacktop had been laid down over it. It was marked on the maps as a bicycle path. Cyclists were already whizzing past the house on weekend afternoons, beneath the white-arching corridor of pylons. The path went on for miles; you could ride it out past the new subdivisions to the west and up through the hills, where on the clearest days you could see the glittering dragon tail of the great river.

One afternoon toward the end of that summer, everyone in the household began collecting supplies for a picnic. They brought out musty old checked woolen blankets from the linen closet and dragged up cobwebbed wicker baskets from the basement; they wrapped up snacks in foil and put bottles of pop in Tupperware tubs filled with ice. The kids watched all these preparations in bewilderment. It was too late in the day for a picnic, and nobody in the house ever went to the drive-in. But nobody would explain what we were doing instead.

The traffic on Troy Road was impossible. It was as if the whole town were being evacuated. Cars were bumper-to-bumper, tops down, radios blaring. People were calling and waving, and teenagers were jumping from car to car. We rode decorously with Eugene and Helen, while Hilda and Marty followed behind. The line crept south past the big floodlit shopping center. Then we sat and stared for what felt like hours at a new drive-through fast-food joint lit up like a neon flying saucer. The glowing scribbles on the sign never tired of spelling out *Char-Co Burgers*. Beyond that were the first open fields and distant hillsides where subdivision windows glimmered in the evening light. Farther on we passed a big intersection with sleek new gas stations and a family restaurant with a blue plastic chalet roof.

Several miles south of town, the line of cars came to a fork in the road. To the left was the original Troy Road, which ran southeast toward the town of Troy, deep in farm country. To the right was a fresh stretch of main highway that cut to the southwest and connected to the interstate. In between these turnings were the fenced-in grounds of an old railroad-tie factory.

The factory had been derelict for years. But that night there were men with flashlights and flares waving the cars in through the open gates. Other men were directing them to park in the clear spaces among the plateaus of broken asphalt and the fields of towering weeds. People were streaming toward the central square. There the weeds and grasses had been cut down enough to allow everyone to spread out their picnic blankets and unfold their lawn chairs. At the far end of the square a wooden platform had been erected, with a big shrouded backdrop behind; there was a bank of loudspeakers massed before it and floodlights on either side.

Thousands of people were there—the whole town, I was certain. Everybody was laughing and shouting to one another.

Kids were scampering everywhere; some were wildly waving around sparklers as though writing messages on the darkening air. Our little enclave was hushed. Eugene and Marty sat silently—dignified, reserved, thoroughly bored, like farmers on their Sunday-best behavior. Hilda was shooting out glares in all directions. She hated how casually everybody in the crowd was dressed, the men in Bermuda shorts and the women in Capri pants. Helen appeared to be in a bad mood because she was looking for someone in the crowd who wasn't there.

The evening was clear, chilly, and windy, the first cool weather of September. The sky overhead was a deepening glassy blue-black that was gradually being speckled by the Milky Way. In the west, after the sunset faded, a huge smear of copper and orange remained on the horizon—that was the mark of the factories and refineries around Saint Louis. To the north were the silhouettes of low, forested hills. They were backlit by a pale phosphorescent halo—the glow of Edwardsville's streetlights, illuminating the deserted town.

The loudspeakers emitted a warning squawk. A hush fell over the crowd. The floodlights snapped on and the shroud slithered away from the backdrop.

The scene showed the Mississippi River valley as it had been a thousand years ago. There were lush forests, rolling hills, and an immense grassy mound looming up against the horizon. This was where a Native American city stood, on the site of present-day Edwardsville. Actors in hand-sewn buckram outfits mounted the platform to recite speeches about the kindliness of the earth and the unstained spirituality of their civilization.

The next scene jumped forward hundreds of years. The new backdrop showed that the forest had reclaimed the land; the city was gone and the current inhabitants no longer knew it had existed. The only trace left was the mysterious mound. The first white explorers arrived and were astonished by the sight of it. They wondered whether it might have been built by refugees from Atlantis or one of the lost tribes of Israel.

In the next scene we saw a man walking down a road. It was our introduction to Ninian Edwards, the founder of Edwardsville. He frequently walked the road to Troy to visit a friend. He thought the land where the Indian city had been would be a fine place for a town. So next we saw him presiding over a treaty in which the last tribal lands on the Illinois side of the Mississippi River were ceded to the whites. And now the construction of Edwardsville could begin.

So it went on, tableau after tableau, as the town was built and its life unfolded over the next century and a half. Crowds of citizens gathered in the town square. Whiskered politicians made speeches about slavery and the Spanish-American War. Battalions of soldiers marched off to Europe. A chorus line of bathing beauties preened. A silhouette of a railroad train disgorged a promenade of visiting celebrities—a finger-fluttery W. C. Fields, a blackfaced Al Jolson. A file of artillery pieces was paraded past. The flag was raised on Iwo Jima. A squad of Legionnaires with real rifles gave a twenty-one-gun salute.

Each new scene set off a wave of recognition from the crowd, a surge of murmuring or a shower of laughter. I kept looking up at my four old relatives to see whether they were following the story. I couldn't tell. They sat silently, arms crossed, as impassive as a row of statues. The glare of the stage lights shone on their glasses and hid their eyes.

At last the pageant reached the present day. The backdrop was lowered to reveal a big pyrotechnic set piece. It was ignited. The brilliant white flares carved out the unmistakable shape of a mushroom cloud. The crowd gasped. Then the flares guttered out into billows of smoke, and everybody applauded.

10

Things They Never Told

CLARENCE AND MARY'S travels with the Airstream trailer ended in western Montana. They were coming down the Rockies one October night in 1967 when they were met by a thundering tanker truck on its way up. The truck took a sharp curve in a contemptuously wide sweep. It roared past the station wagon and sideswiped the trailer. Then it went grinding on up into the mountains without a pause.

The station wagon fishtailed wildly; the trailer broke loose from the hitch. Clarence and Mary were spun around sickeningly before the wagon came to rest on the highway shoulder. The trailer careened past them, caromed off the slope, swerved back through the glare of their headlights, and vanished.

It was a moonless night. When they stood on the shoulder and pointed their flashlight down into the blackness, they couldn't make out much more than the sheen of dented aluminum and a scattering of clothes draped over a scrub tree below. They were miles from the nearest town and there was no traffic on the road in either direction. They decided there was nothing they could do until daylight.

They checked into a motel on the outskirts of a town at the base of the foothills. Neither of them could sleep. They went out before dawn and found a twenty-four-hour diner at a truck stop down the road. They sat in a window booth and watched the sun come up. Then they talked about what they should do next.

They had insurance; the first step was to call the adjuster. Clarence was pretty sure their policy would cover the cost of another trailer. But he hesitated—or else, while he was talking, Mary involuntarily made a face. Afterward neither of them could remember which it was. But it didn't matter. Either way, they were thinking the same thing. They didn't want to replace the Airstream. They were done with being on the road.

Later that morning, they drove back into the hills to take a look at the trailer. It was lying at the bottom of a deep gully. Its frame was bent and its aluminum skin had ruptured. It looked like a deflated hot-air balloon. The "Sta-Closed" latches had all burst open, and their belongings were scattered up and down the slope: clothes, dishes, wading boots, painting supplies, canned foods, decks of playing cards, clip-on lamp shades, fishing tackle, silverware, unspooling reels of Super 8 film, bottles of mouthwash and deodorant and shampoo.

Clarence climbed down and spent a couple of hours scooping up whatever seemed like worthwhile salvage. It was barely enough to fill the backseat of the station wagon.

One treasure he refused to leave behind: his new portable TV. Mary looked at him like he was a lunatic when she saw him lugging it up the ridge. The set hadn't just fallen among the rocks of the gully; some of the contents of the kitchen cabinets had gone bouncing down along with it. Jars of peanut butter and jelly and honey had cracked open over its chassis, and their contents had dripped into its interior. But it was expensive; he hated to abandon it without getting a professional opinion.

Back in town, they cruised along the main street until they came to a small storefront with a hand-painted sign in the window that said *We Fix Everything Electrical*. The display was a clutter of dusty vacuum cleaners, fans that looked like prehistoric fossils, and Bakelite radios. Clarence showed the TV to the store owner. He was intrigued; he set it down on his workbench and plugged it in. The picture tube slowly came to life. He offered to buy it on the spot.

Afterward Clarence and Mary went for a stroll. It was a golden autumn afternoon; they walked till they came to the edge of town. The sidewalk ended at a little park with a stone bench. They sat for a while and watched a stand of poplars on the other side of the park shedding leaves into the wind. The land beyond the town was brown and empty; as the afternoon faded, a few remote lights began glimmering in the hills.

Clarence asked Mary where, if she could pick anyplace they'd been, she'd like to settle down for good. She answered immediately. Afterward she would never admit whether this was really where she wanted to go or whether she was just saying it because she knew it would please him: the Florida Keys.

They left town a couple of days later. As they headed off down the main street toward the interstate, they passed the appliance store. Their TV was now given pride of place in the window. There was a big sign that read:

THIS ZENITH TV HAS PEANUT
BUTTER AND JELLY INSIDE IT
AND IT STILL WORKS.

Clarence and Mary bought a house on Big Pine Key, one of the larger islands in the chain. The Keys were still sparsely settled then; many islets were untouched, and a few seemed barely even observed. But Big Pine Key did have some signs of human occupancy—there was a little cluster of houses and commercial buildings near the main highway that passed for a town; there was even a post office and a general store. The house that Clarence and Mary found was on the beach, down a dirt road off the main highway. It was a hot, windy, sun-dazzled spot. Only a few other houses were within walking distance. The most prominent local landmark was a canal down the shoreline where alligators congregated to sun themselves.

Just as soon as Clarence and Mary were settled in, they resumed their old routine. Clarence got up before dawn each day and went out fishing in a little outboard boat. Mary would find a picturesque spot, of which there was no shortage, where she could work on her paintings. As she explored, she grew fascinated by all the things that washed up on the beaches—the stones and shells, the drift glass and driftwood. She started collecting the odder pieces of driftwood, and then she got the idea to paint on them. She did a whole series of little paintings, of fishing boats silhouetted against tropical sunsets and pelicans perched on battered old piers.

Every few months, she'd go into Key West and sell her latest work at art fairs. The driftwood paintings were an immediate hit—she sold them all in a couple of hours. After that, she gave up painting on canvas and collected all the driftwood she could find. Pretty soon she started running short; she'd scoured all the beaches on the key and had to venture to the other keys to find more. She decided it would be easier to make her own. So she set up a big tub of salt water in her backyard, filled it with pieces of wooden crates that she'd smashed up with an ax, and soaked them until they looked like they might have been tumbling around in the groundswell for years.

One winter my parents and I went to Big Pine Key for a visit. Mary proved to be flourishing. She was relaxed, tanned, and cheerful, with little trace left of her old waspishness. She had become a big local success as a painter; she sold every drift-wood painting she made, people all over the Keys recognized her, and she'd been written up once in a Key West newspaper. She was friends with everybody on Big Pine Key. Her best friends were a retired military couple who lived down the shore in a new beach house; Mary liked to walk over there in the afternoons to play cards and argue about Nixon and Vietnam. (Mary, like the rest of that generation of the family, was a fierce lifelong Democrat.)

Clarence wasn't doing as well. He was just as tanned as Mary, but somehow his skin looked pasty and unhealthy. He was vague and irritable and he constantly complained, mainly about how the Keys were being ruined by overdevelopment. He moved with difficulty, and his chronic cough was getting worse. But he still tried to muster a great show of vigor, and one day he insisted on taking me out fishing.

We spent hours together in silence, as the boat puttered and drifted past reefs and lush coves and deserted islets. The water was pale blue and aquamarine, and it was so clear that I could see carpets of bulging sponges twenty or thirty feet below us. All the while, Clarence stared out at the ocean and his fishing lines with absolute concentration. I wanted to say something to him—but I had no idea what. At last I opened my mouth and blurted out the first words that came to me. I asked whether it was true that as you got older, time passed more quickly.

He regarded me in astonishment. It was as though he'd

never heard such an idea before. He looked out for a long time over the ruffled water. Finally he said, "Well, the years do go by like a rocket. But the days just get longer and longer."

Hilda was diagnosed with colon cancer at the end of 1968. Her first impulse was to keep the news to herself. Serious illness wasn't something you discussed openly back then, and the word "cancer" was completely taboo; this was a time, after all, when skittish astrologers renamed those born under the sign of Cancer "Moon Children." So Hilda made her doctor's appointments in strictest secrecy and scheduled them for times when the rest of the household was gone and she could drive downtown to the doctor's office unobserved. She might even have tried to keep the surgery itself secret if she hadn't been worried about Marty.

A week before she was scheduled to go to the hospital, she knew the time was up and she had to talk to Eugene and Helen. So, one rainy weekend afternoon, she sat them both down at the dining room table and explained her condition. She said that the doctor believed her chances were good. She herself was skeptical—she remembered how Bosh had died. But that didn't matter. The important thing was that she wanted a promise from both of them: if she didn't survive, they would let Marty go on living in the house.

They all sat silently. The rain poured down; the big clock in the hallway tocked. Then Eugene pushed up from the table and left the room without saying a word. Helen sat with her head bowed. Hilda at last got up and started busily straightening the stacks of Helen's magazines on the sideboard. She knew that they had agreed.

Nothing more was said about it, then or later. If Marty himself ever had any inkling of the deal, he gave no sign.

Hilda's surgery and its aftermath left her weak and exhausted. The news went out to the family that there could be no visits from the children that summer. The word "cancer" was never mentioned; we were told she had anemia. So instead of going to Edwardsville I spent a radiantly happy summer hanging out with my friends at home, playing baseball in familiar fields and swimming in local park-district pools. Edwardsville wasn't mentioned the next summer, either, or the summer after that, and I don't think I ever noticed. I just assumed that Edwardsville was now part of the past.

The doctor proclaimed Hilda's treatment a success. But she never did come all the way back. She lost her vigor and from then on was tired out after the least exertion. Still, she forced herself back into her old habits, cooking and cleaning with a hint of her former gusto. She didn't think she had a choice; only an immoral layabout would be kept in bed by illness.

The rest of the household followed her lead—Marty especially. He barely acknowledged that she'd been unwell. He still expected her to fetch his newspaper and serve him dinner and wash out his underwear the way she always had. In general he gave the impression that her cancer was mainly an imposition on him.

Eugene watched Marty's treatment of Hilda with gathering rage. One afternoon, at Eugene's instigation, the two men carried a small couch upstairs so Hilda could sit at ease at the window if she was feeling too weak to leave her bedroom. Midway through their maneuvers up the back stairs, Eugene realized that he was doing all the heavy work while Marty was putting on a great pantomime of groaning effort over nothing. The moment they set the couch down, Eugene punched Marty in the face. Marty fell backward onto the couch and began bawling. Eugene landed several more blows on his face and in his belly. Then he grabbed Marty by the throat and squeezed. Marty stared at him in bug-eyed terror. Then Eugene let go and clumped back down the stairs.

Marty's face was left badly scratched and bruised by the fight with Eugene, and he had to get new glasses to replace the pair that had been smashed. But he uncharacteristically refused to look for sympathy. He didn't even invent a story to explain his appearance. For weeks afterward he avoided Eugene; he averted his gaze when they sat together at the dinner table. Only gradually and cautiously did he resume his old round of heavy joshing.

But this time Eugene didn't respond. He didn't become red faced and silently furious, the way he'd always done; he didn't react at all. From then on, he behaved as though Marty didn't exist. If Marty addressed a direct question to him, Eugene pretended not to hear it. If Marty asked for or offered something at the dinner table, Eugene ignored him. If Marty met him in the hallway, Eugene shouldered past him—sometimes knocking him into the coatrack or against the umbrella stand without a word of apology. Soon Eugene was refusing to use or touch anything in the house that was associated with Marty in any way. This was a problem at dinner, because the table was still being set with the flatware Marty had brought back from the navy. But Eugene arrived at a solution. He ordered his own set of black-handled silverware from a mail-order catalog and ostentatiously set it out at his own place each night.

The few people who visited the household in those days noticed what Eugene was doing, and they would wonder how long he could keep it up. Surely even he couldn't sustain this charade indefinitely; sooner or later he'd have to crack. But he never did. As far as anybody could tell, Eugene didn't say another word to Marty for the next seventeen years.

Helen continued to acknowledge Marty's presence—reluctantly, and always in tones of sarcasm and contempt. She refused to be alone with him. She wouldn't accept his help with chores on those rare occasions when he offered it. She never laughed at his jokes; the most she'd permit herself was a disgusted sniff whenever he said anything she considered particularly stupid. She was consumed by a ceaseless rage at the sheer thought of his existence. The slightest sound he made from the parlor—the flutter of a dropped newspaper section, the sucking on a fresh cigar—would make her flinch as though she'd heard a gunshot.

So this was how it went in the house from then on. During the days, Helen was at work; Eugene was either puttering in the garden or sleeping in his bedroom with the door locked. Marty and Hilda had the place to themselves. Mornings, Marty would sit in his chair in the parlor and read the papers; Hilda would clean the house. Afternoons, Marty would often go off somewhere—he never said where, and Hilda never asked. Hilda would sag into her chair in the kitchen and sit in exhaustion till it was time to cook dinner.

The evening was the only time the four of them were together in the same room. They'd sit around the oak table and eat in silence. The TV was left on in the parlor, and Hilda or Helen would sometimes crane her head to listen to something on the news. The only other sounds were their breaths and sighs and grunts, the clack of teeth and the smack of lips, the clicks of the flatware and the thunks of the plates. They would pass the bowls and platters and pitchers and the salt and pepper shakers from hand to hand like chess masters playing a lightning round.

Afterward, Hilda would clear away the table. Eugene would head off to work—he was still on the graveyard shift. Marty would sit back down in the parlor, flip through the evening papers, and smoke a cigar. Then he'd trudge up the stairs to bed. Hilda would join him after she'd finished washing the dishes and cleaned up the newspapers he had left scattered around his chair.

Helen was left alone. She'd sit at the dining room table and play a few games of solitaire while idly listening to the TV. Then she'd shut off the TV and the lights and go into her bedroom. And there, every night, she'd get down on her knees at the bedside and pray that Marty would die before Hilda so she wouldn't have to keep her promise.

Clarence died in the spring of 1973, at a hospital in Miami. The cause of death was emphysema. The family had his body brought back to Edwardsville to be buried.

Eugene retired from the Wood River refinery in 1977. He soon found that he couldn't bear to be in the house day after day. It wasn't just Marty; he hated being idle. But his gardens were flourishing by themselves, and too often now he couldn't find anything to do with them that wasn't busywork. So he started leaving the house whenever the weather was warm. He'd take a bag lunch with him (invariably a bologna sandwich and an apple) and he'd walk up Troy Road to town.

By that point, the dominant presence in Edwardsville was Southern Illinois University. It was a huge campus sprawling over the countryside to the west, with a student body of twelve thousand—more people than lived in Edwardsville itself. Its students and faculty were everywhere. The rows of old storefronts downtown were occupied by chain clothing outlets, fast-food restaurants, record stores, and coffeehouses; when you walked down any side street, you'd hear rock music floating down from attic windows, and you'd smell marijuana mingling with the scent of the lilac bushes.

Eugene could even see it on Troy Road. The university had taken over the Nelson company complex, which had stood derelict for decades. The brass foundry had been assigned to the art department and had been refurbished as studio space for student artists. The big doors were left standing open on warm days; if you peered inside, you found that the great sky-lighted hall was now a warren of cluttered cubbyholes that smelled of clay and plaster and lath. A couple of blocks north was the old clapboard building that had once been Sehnert's Hotel; it had been occupied, too. It was now a hamburger tavern, with rooms to rent upstairs to grad students. Every time Eugene passed it, it was throbbing with a rock bass line like a toothache.

But there were places where the feel of the old Edwardsville still lingered. One of them was the big park opposite the town hall. That was where Eugene's walks usually ended up. The park's magnificent old elms had died in the blight, but there were still towering oaks and maples and willows and sycamores, and new trees had been planted to replace those that had been lost—ashes, catalpas, and gingkos. There were paths weaving in and out of the groves, and here and there were stone tables where old men sat and talked and played checkers and chess. And there were several secluded benches where you could sit for as long as you wanted without anyone bothering you. Eugene spent his afternoons placidly catching up on his seed catalogs.

At first, the other regulars in the park left him alone. But the same people kept showing up day after day, summer after summer, and gradually, insensibly, he fell into the habit of nodding at those he recognized. When he was feeling especially social, he'd sit on the outskirts of the circle that gathered around the chessboards. Once in a while, somebody would dare to say hello to him. Eventually he began to grunt a hello back.

Against his will, he grew fascinated by their talk. Most

of the regulars were veterans and had served in World War II or in Korea. Eugene had never spent any time with fellow veterans before and was surprised to hear them describe matter-of-factly things he thought he alone had experienced. So, one day, to his own great surprise, he found himself telling the group about a scene he had witnessed in the Marshall Islands. A fiercely defended coastline had been pulverized by a day-long barrage of naval artillery; when he and his team had gone ashore, they'd found nothing for a mile inland but splinters of palm trees and threads of human flesh.

He had expected his listeners to be shocked; they just nodded ruefully. So next he talked about what had happened on Saipan. Once the island had been taken, there were dozens of Japanese soldiers who refused to emerge from the bolt-holes they'd dug into the hillsides, so Eugene and the other Seabees had simply and methodically bulldozed over the entrances. Then they tried to deal with the hundreds of Japanese civilians still on the island. But they'd thrown themselves off the cliffs rather than surrender.

His listeners nodded at those stories, too. They'd all been through things as bad or worse.

So at last he told them about how his time in the combat zone had ended.

It had happened on Saipan, in the summer of 1944. One night a Japanese soldier on a suicide run broke through the American lines near the airfield, triggering a storm of gunfire and mortar shells shooting off in all directions. It was the sort of thing they'd endured every night—but for some reason this time it was too much for Eugene. As he waited it out in his foxhole, he began sobbing uncontrollably. He didn't stop after the all-clear. He was still gasping and wailing and crying when he was brought into the aid station. By the time he'd reached the base hospital he'd fallen silent. He felt no need to speak or make eye contact with anyone. A long voyage had followed, to a military hospital in Australia, and afterward to a stateside hospital near Yosemite. His treatment was not tender. There were relentless sessions of electroshock and massive injections of insulin. It took years—but eventually the doctors did succeed in brutalizing him into speaking again.

When Eugene was finished telling that story, some wall in his mind seemed to come down. He didn't relapse back into his customary silence; he went on talking. From then on, every day at the park, he talked to whoever showed up. Then he started talking to Hilda and Helen at home. The dinner table was no longer silent; instead it became the place where, each night, Eugene would hold forth. Oblivious to whether the other people there were interested or even listening, he'd spill out talk from a lifetime's reserve: about being on the bum during the Depression, about hunting and whoring with Uncle August and Uncle Frank, about Bougainville and the Solomons and Saipan. "It was amazing," says his niece Dorothy. "Suddenly you couldn't shut him up."

Mostly he talked about gardening. He had countless stories about his against-all-odds triumphs and inexplicable failures, about his risky ordering of rare bulbs from obscure catalogs, about his ceaseless worries as to whether this season the zinnias or the sunflowers would flourish. Shade and sun, seeds and peat, forced bulbs and fertilizer and topsoil—it was a gargantuan flow, an unreeling Mississippi of gardening lore that was silenced only by the fatal heart attack he suffered on New Year's Day, 1986.

The next spring, Marty took over Eugene's gardens. He proved to be an untalented but conscientious caretaker. He didn't bother to replace any of the annuals, and he let some of the frailer perennials die. But he faithfully watered and pruned and weeded even in the hottest summers. The gardens retained much of their beauty for several years.

He was surprised and touched when visitors complimented him on his success. But he was quick to say that all the credit belonged to Eugene. He invariably spoke of Eugene with respect. It was as though he had forgotten their feud—or else had never been aware of it in the first place. Sometimes when he came to the dinner table after a hard afternoon in the gardens, he would declare, "I just don't know how he did it all. That man must have been some kind of dynamo."

Then one spring something happened. Marty couldn't work in the gardens anymore. By summer he could barely move or speak. When people visited the house, his face brightened and he rose up to shake hands with a hint of his customary enthusiasm—but he was visibly baffled by who everybody was, and he'd quickly sink back into his chair and refuse to say another word.

As he lapsed into complete passivity, Hilda spent all her time caring for him. She brushed his hair and dressed him in the mornings. She served him his lunches on a TV tray. She fetched his newspapers, even though he didn't do more than glance at them before letting them fall to the carpet. She left the TV on in the parlor all day whether or not he made any sign of watching it.

Helen, meanwhile, provided him with company: a big framed photograph she placed on the parlor mantel. It was a rare shot somebody had taken of Eugene. It was in the gardens, and it showed Eugene turning toward the camera and regarding the photographer with surprise and anger. Helen positioned it right in front of the armchair, so that every time Marty looked up, he'd see Eugene glaring at him.

But Marty made no sign of noticing. He never remarked on the photo, or anything else. He sat silently, bothering no one and making no fuss, until the day in 1993 when Helen's prayers were answered and he died in his sleep.

Helen and Hilda stayed on in the house together. They played out an endless vaudeville routine of intimate bickering. They made sour faces at each other's jokes, and they cut short each other's favorite stories, and they snapped at each other over long-standing grievances invisible to outsiders. They argued about everything, from the correct oven temperature for pot roast to the exact alignment of the TV antenna. Every evening, they'd sit at the kitchen table and watch the TV in the parlor; their favorite show was *Wheel of Fortune*, and they'd argue furiously about the best way to watch it. Hilda insisted on calling out the solutions as they occurred to her, while Helen wanted to solve them silently on her own.

They also maintained the house's tradition of hospitality, after their fashion. My cousin Bill, who was working then for Boeing in Saint Louis, would sometimes drive over for weekend visits. He remembers: "They had this idea fixed in their minds: young men like soda pop. So whenever I showed up they'd have bottles of soda pop waiting for me on the kitchen table. It was some local brand I'd never heard of, orange or grape or something. It was completely flat, like they'd kept it in the basement for twenty years. It was awful. But they also had this weird sixth sense about visitors. If I came by myself, then I had to stay out of the parlor, because the parlor was for guests. But if I brought a friend along, they somehow knew beforehand, and everything was already set up in the parlor for us."

Then they would begin to pester him with shrewd questions regarding Boeing and its troubles. They were up on all the financial news; they'd become huge fans of CNN.

Bill remembers: "They obviously cared a lot for each other. They seemed very self-sufficient, like they wouldn't want to live any other way. But there was this one time, after I was married, when I brought my wife and our new baby daughter Kayla. Hilda just scooped Kayla up and handled her like she was born to do it. I remember thinking then that it was strange she'd never had children of her own."

A year or so after Marty died, Hilda at last told Helen the true story of her marriage. Hilda said that when she'd first met Marty, more than fifty years earlier, he'd been having an affair with a woman he'd known from Wehrle's grocery store. The woman was married; it had been her idea for Marty to take up with Hilda, just to provide them with camouflage.

Hilda herself had never been deceived. She'd known all about Marty and the other woman from the beginning. She'd gone along with it, not because she loved Marty—she never had cared for him much—but because she'd wanted children, and because after all those years she'd spent tending house for her grandmother, she thought she was too old to find a real husband. So Hilda and Marty had made a deal: they would get married, and she would ignore his affair, in exchange for children and a home of her own.

But after Marty got back from the war, he reneged on all of it. He said there was no reason for them to spend money on a house when they had free rent where they were. He said he had no interest whatever in having children; he could barely tolerate the summertime visits from her nieces and nephews.

He said that he was too old and set in his ways to change, and she should have figured this out before she married him. And that was that.

Hilda's health began to fail again. Helen described it in a letter:

> *Hilda is almost blind—has macular degeneration in both eyes. Also had her ear with cancer so she has to have an operation so can hear sometimes. Beside that she had her toenails cut and the gal must have cut too deep as she has an infection in her big toe. I'm glad I am here to keep her. But as you see the golden years aren't so golden.*

In the last year of her life, Hilda became aware of an unseen presence in the house. She took to sitting in Marty's old chair in the parlor, where she would spend hours listening for its signs. She grew attuned to obscure noises: an unexplained bump on the stairs, the surreptitious creak of the floorboards, the rustle of curtains across a shut window. Gradually, in the corners of her eyes, she began to make out a figure standing silently in dark doorways and at the far side of empty rooms.

It never spoke or moved. It seemed to be in shadow even when the sunlight fell on it directly. When she squinted hard at it, it melted away. But she had no doubt about its identity. It was Bosh, watching sorrowfully over his children as he had always done.

This Is All I Know

HILDA DIED IN the summer of 1996, and after that Helen had the house to herself. She stayed inside and kept the blinds drawn. Sometimes she spent whole days in her favorite spot at the dining room table, playing solitaire and watching TV through the parlor door. She had no company but her dog, Babe.

Babe was a foul-tempered, badly behaved schnauzer. Helen regarded him with unfailing love. She was never happier than when she could chatter about his doings. In one letter she wrote:

The postman just came & Babe had a fit I'm surprised you can't hear him bark. He's so loud & runs back & forth around the house. I have barricades over most doors so he is confined to the dining room kitchen & back bedroom. I still have Valentine candy I never opened as he is right there & shouldn't have chocolate.

She paid no attention to the condition of the house. The kitchen filled with garbage bags, and there were avalanches of magazines in the parlor. The carpets and rugs were all stained with dog droppings and urine. Whenever visitors managed to talk their way past the front door, they were shocked by the state of the place. They'd sometimes ask Helen what Agnes or Hilda would have thought. "They enjoyed doing housework," Helen said. "I don't."

The gardens were a brilliant shambles, gradually conquered by bindweed and kudzu. She wrote:

I can't plant anything. I just enjoy what comes up.

Occasionally she did venture outside. Usually she went out the back gate and crossed beneath the power pylons to First Avenue. Her friend Irene lived there; she was alone in her old family home just the way Helen was.

There wasn't much left by then of their neighborhood. The area had been rezoned for light industry, and most of the old houses had vanished. The ones that survived were shabby and down-at-the-heels; the clapboard needed paint, the picket fences were sagging, and they had carcasses of pickup trucks squatting on cinder blocks in their yards.

Everywhere was new construction. There was now a truck lot on Second Avenue: a fenced-in plain of asphalt, floodlit at night, where row after row of big rigs were squatting. Across the street was an agricultural supply company that always had huge hulking tanks of chemical fertilizer stacked on its loading dock. Next door was an industrial finishing plant that constantly emitted the shrieks and whines of tortured metal. Looming over everything at the far end of the block was a radio tower; the pulsing red light at its peak could be seen at night for miles away.

Sometimes Helen got in her car and drove down Troy Road. The land there was getting crowded, too. The roadside south of Second Avenue was lined by mini-malls and franchise strips, auto parts dealers and discount furniture warehouses, franchise restaurants and cell phone dealers and fly-by-night computer repair storefronts, on and on for miles. It was part of the immense wave of exurban development that was spreading out and thickening around metropolitan St. Louis.

Helen's goal was the new Kmart. She liked that store and was always fretting about the reports she heard on CNN regarding Kmart's finances. *They are in trouble all over*, she wrote in a letter. *I'd hate to see them go.*

Her car was just mobile enough to get her to Kmart and back again: it was a thirty-year-old Chevy Malibu. She bristled whenever anybody told her to replace it. She wrote:

I don't care to have a new car. I'm sentimental about things.

Helen was diagnosed with non-Hodgkin's lymphoma in November of 1999. She was under no illusions about her chances. She was eighty-six and had been extremely frail for several years; she knew that any operation would most likely kill her. Her only concern was to find a new home for Babe. Once she succeeded in getting a friend of a friend to adopt him, she was ready.

The hospital was on the far side of town near the university. It was a sleek hulk of red brick, with stylized turrets and battlements, like a postmodernist version of a Victorian factory. Helen's room was on the top floor. When she roused herself to go to the window, she had a view of the busy commercial street below, and in the distance, new rows of town houses and the university campus to the west.

She had a lot of visitors. When the word spread that she was sick, her nieces and some of her grandnieces and grandnephews drove down from Chicago. Many of them hadn't been in Edwardsville in decades. It became a low-key, ongoing family reunion. The sounds of talk and soft laughter came floating out from her room day after day, while the other open doors along the corridor were emitting hisses and beeps and clicks and the drone of Jerry Springer and *The People's Court*.

Helen mostly passed the time by complaining. She ruminated endlessly over past wounds—especially Marty's refusal to go away. She talked about Marty constantly. She told all her visitors about his infidelities and betrayals and his abysmal treatment of Hilda. She brightened only when she remembered how he had been beaten up by Eugene. One time she described the afternoon, forty years before, when he had tried to kiss her; the memory made her so angry that the nurses rushed in to find out what was wrong. She even blamed Marty for the poor condition of the property. She was particularly bitter about the picket fence, which was the original turn-of-the-century cypress and badly rotted. "That man went in and out the gate ten times a day," she said. "He wore it out."

Some of her visitors tried to change the subject. They began talking about how much the house had meant to them over the years. At first she refused to believe them. It had never occurred to her that anyone had cared about the house at all. She listened openmouthed while people reminisced about the games of "Movie Stars" on the front porch, the solemn dishwashing after dinner, and the group peach-peeling on high summer afternoons. When someone described running frantically to retrieve the white sheets from the laundry lines before the trains passed, she laughed out loud.

Then somebody asked her to talk about her own favorite memories. She got angry and said that nobody ought to care about those times any longer.

Later that night, after the last of the visitors had departed, Helen asked a nurse for paper and a pen. She wrote at the top of a page:

I will tell you of our family.

She didn't try to record a connected story. She just wrote a phrase or two describing what she remembered about her relatives as they rose up in her mind—looks, gestures, stray facts, lingering details. She began with her grandfather and his hotel in Pierron, offering "fit entertainment for man and beast." Then she skipped on to her father and his job at the Nelson brass foundry. Then there were her grandmother's people in Alhambra, and the factory fire that was no accident. Then there was her uncle Frank and his horrible eczema and its mysterious cure. There was a cousin Herman; he had beautiful brown eyes and dimples. There was an uncle Emil who was going to be a druggist, but he couldn't stand the stink of the chemicals; he became a grocer instead. There was another cousin who ran a store, went broke, and became a very good salesman. *He had the gift of gab*, Helen wrote, *and that's what it takes.*

So she kept scribbling on, that night and the nights that followed, filling up pages haphazardly, glancing at lives passed in remote farms and obscure villages and dusty market towns, sparing a few words each for train conductors and telephone operators, seamstresses and land surveyors, gandy dancers and oil field workers, bachelor uncles and spinster aunts and drunken grandfathers and agoraphobic widows—a whole lost world of marriage vows kept, mortgages paid off, jobs held until retirement, deaths at home surrounded by children and grandchildren, a world as green and placid as the life at the bottom of a deep still pond.

On the last page she came to her own generation:

Clarence was the only one of us who finished high school. He worked at the Radiator Mfg. Co., then sold Real Silk Hosiery before going to Chicago to earn his fortune and lady love.

Pearl Bilyeu finished eighth grade before going to N.O. Nelson to work as a packer. There she met Cecil and married.

Hilda Martindale had three years of high school and didn't like it so quit.

Eugene had a lot of jobs, depression time and you couldn't hardly find a job so he took anything. He was our handyman, gardener, plumber, etc.

Helen (that's me) finished 2 years high school. Went to work after Pop died. Made dresses until I retired after 47 years of work. Long time, huh!

Underneath she wrote:

This is all I know.

After Helen died, the family cleaned out the house. They donated the furniture to Goodwill and sent all the clothes and dishware to a church rummage sale. The heirlooms and mementos were distributed among a scattering of relatives and family friends. The one memento that everybody wanted was the framed photo of Eugene that had stood on the mantel. But it was nowhere to be found. A joke went around that Bosh must have taken it.

The family then hired a Realtor to appraise the property. He wasn't sanguine about its prospects. The house suffered, he wrote, from both functional and economic obsolescence. By functional obsolescence he meant its old-fashioned design; by economic obsolescence he meant the neighborhood. He thought it extremely unlikely that anybody would want to live in the house even if it were thoroughly rehabbed. He estimated its fair market value to be $50,000—chump change in Edwardsville's booming real estate market.

His conclusion was phrased in the traditional language of his trade: *In my opinion, the Highest and Best use for this property is for a parking lot.*

At the end of the next winter, just before the house was put on the market, my wife and I went down to Edwardsville for a visit. It was a dreary March afternoon; the sky was gunmetal gray. The house was closed up. The picket fence was a ruin; the windows on the back porch were broken; the hand pump by the kitchen door was rusted shut. There were skeletal trellises standing here and there in the flower beds, swaying and rattling in the wind. The scene was like a daguerreotype in a history book—a pioneer homestead abandoned at the edge of the wilderness.

My wife had brought a set of garden tools along with her, and she spent a couple of hours excavating every root and bulb she could find in the gardens. It was hard, frustrating work; many of Eugene's prizes remained hidden. His beloved tulips were so deeply buried, it would have taken a steam shovel to unearth them. But she did come away with a big sack of smelly, earth-caked salvage.

When we got back home to Chicago, she planted the pick of the bulbs in her gardens. The rest she gave away to friends around our neighborhood. That spring, the yards and parkways and corner plots for blocks around were spangled with Eugene's zinnias and snapdragons and bee balm. But there was one root she set aside. We took it to one of the old railroad corridors and planted it along the slope below the tracks in Eugene's memory.

We went by there again in September. It was a beautiful afternoon, the first cool day of fall. The tracks ran on as far as we could see—a glinting double line merging and vanishing among the remote blue silhouettes of treetops and apartment blocks. The slopes were a rich tangle of grasses and weeds and prairie wildflowers. When we came to the spot we remembered, we found a frail white aster in bloom.

The Protestant cemetery on the outskirts of Edwardsville is always referred to in my family as "the new cemetery"—distinguishing it from the old Catholic cemetery on the opposite side of town, where Bosh and Agnes and our earlier ancestors are buried. The new cemetery looks pretty much like the old one. But it does have a small chapel built in the austere modernist style that's been popular for religious architecture in the last several decades: a stark A-frame of blond wood, steel, and clear glass, unadorned and sparsely furnished, looking less like a place of worship than a lobby at NASA.

In March 2000 the family gathered at the chapel. Sehnert cousins, second cousins, children and grandchildren and great-grandchildren sat in the pews silently, discreetly unzipping coats, muffling coughs, hushing the chirp of cell phones. Through the glass behind the altar, we could see slow veils and billows of mist drifting across the trees, and the air was filled with the gurgles and taps of dripping water; heavy rains had fallen the night before, the first soaking rains of spring.

Beside the pulpit was a card table on which framed photos had been set up. There was my grandmother Mary as a child, on the stoop of her elm-shaded Ravenswood brownstone; Mary as a stylishly plump teenager with a pageboy cut; Mary and Clarence in riding duds, sprawled in the roots of an immense old tree in Lincoln Park. There was a whole series of photos from their time on the road, of Mary with salt-and-pepper hair, standing languidly in front of blurry mountains and looming national forests. There was another series from Mary's decades-long widowhood in the Florida Keys: a white-haired and fiercely tanned retiree, cheerful and alone.

The minister mounted the pulpit. He was a young man in an expensive, poorly fitting suit. Somebody said he'd just arrived in town; he seemed distinctly ill at ease in front of this room of strangers. But as he spoke the familiar words his confidence grew and his voice took on a rich, rolling, backcountry cadence:

"Now is Chrayst rissen from the day-ed, and become the first fruits of thaym that slay-ept. . . ."

After the service, we left the chapel and walked down to the grave site. Ancient headstones loomed up on either side of the path, huddled together here and there in the fog like village skylines. The path led down a steep slope through the trees into a secluded little valley. The rains had churned up the soil, and there were gouts and smears of fresh mud trailing across the path—the orange, odorous, clayey mud of the Mississippi River valley. You could tell that none of us lived in the country from the gingerly manner we picked our way down, frequently stopping to scrape the bright mud from our nice shoes, wincing with distaste as though we'd stepped in animal droppings.

The family plot was on the valley floor, beneath a gaunt

old pine, right where the clusters of headstones ended and the path trailed off into a wide meadow. We gathered in a ragged circle. The markers weren't arranged in a neat row but in a scattered heap, as though they'd tumbled down the slope together. I read the familiar names: Clarence Sehnert, Eugene Sehnert, Helen Sehnert, Earnest C. Martindale, Hilda Martindale. No ornamental headstones, no epitaphs: just the names and dates. I wondered whether any stranger inspecting them would even have a clue how these people were all related to one another.

My uncle Bob came forward and laid the urn containing Mary's ashes on a blanket spread out next to Clarence's marker. No one spoke. After a few moments the wind began to pick up; the fog started to unravel; the tree above us emitted a loud creak. There was an odd involuntary rustle in the group, like the anticipatory flutter in a flock of pigeons.

Without a word, we all turned and started back up the slope. I found myself beside an elderly woman bundled in a thick worn coat. She was having some difficulty on the uneven ground. I gave her my arm and introduced myself.

She looked at me carefully and then shook her head. "No, sorry, I don't remember you. You must forgive me. But there were so many children in that house over the years."

"That's all right," I said. "Were you a neighbor?"

"Oh, heavens, yes. We lived across the train tracks from them all my life. I knew everybody in that family. Even old Bosh. Long before your time. Did you ever hear them talk about him?"

"Sometimes," I said.

She said, "He was quite a character. Every weekend he'd get all duded up and promenade into town to shoot pool. The whole neighborhood would watch him go by. And everybody'd say, 'Come quick; come look at that old drunk in his Sunday best.' Meaning no harm, you know. He'd just laugh anyway if he heard us. And then he got so sick in the end. He had a horrible death, just horrible.

"And I knew Eugene, too, but Eugene, he didn't like to have anything to do with girls. When we were walking home from school my girlfriends and I would always tease him and say we were his valentines, and he'd get all red. Sometimes he'd throw stones at us and sometimes he'd just run away."

The pressure of her hand on my arm was as light as a bird's nest.

She said, "But Helen was my special friend. My dearest friend. After her mother, Agnes, died, Helen and I started traveling together. We went everywhere. She could afford to do it, you know, because she was such a skinflint. I think she saved every penny she ever made, back to all those dreadful old shirt-factory jobs in the Depression. We went on bus tours all over the place, to Nashville and Kansas City and New Orleans."

Then she laughed and looked sideways at me. "But one thing about Helen: she was a complainer. You never heard anybody go on like her. No matter where we went, all the way there and back, she'd be on about everything. The food was too spicy. The beds were too lumpy. And the service! You'd think there wasn't a waitress or a chambermaid with a civil tongue in her head between here and the Mississippi delta."

She fell silent for a moment. Her eyes were fixed on the muddy path rising before us.

She said, "Of course, the moment we'd get home, I'd barely put my feet up before she'd be knocking on the door again, clutching some magazine and showing me a big color picture and saying, 'Here, here, here's where we ought to go next.'"

We reached the top of the ridge. She hung back as the rest of the party drifted on toward the parking lot. She turned to me, but her eyes didn't quite meet mine, as though I were blocking her view of something else.

She said, "Helen and I were inseparable. You know people got so used to seeing us together, they called us Mutt and Jeff. And in all those years we only had one fight. I knew these two men at work and I thought Helen and I should double-date them. They were all right, I thought. Eager beavers, I guess you could say. Kind of dull, but eager to please. They were perfect gentlemen. They took us to a fancy place for dinner and then to a movie. I don't think Helen said six words the whole night. I could tell she was hopping mad. And sure enough, just as soon as we were alone she told me never, ever to do anything like that again. She said if I did, she swore it would be the last I'd ever hear from her for the rest of her life."

She shook her head.

"And I believed her, too. I never did do it again. It was just her and me from then on."

Then she turned away and looked back down into the valley.

"And now there she is. I wish I could visit her more often. But I'm an old woman, and I can't be expected to hike up and down a hill like this just to go see some grave."

The wind strengthened. In the valley below us, pale shafts of sunlight were drifting across the graves and moving out into the swaying meadow grass.

She said, "I never will understand why they picked such a remote spot. But wasn't it just like them?"

Afterword

HEILONGJIANG

MUCH LATER THAN all this, in the city of Harbin, in northern China, I spent an afternoon with a friend who wanted to improve her English. There weren't many people in that part of China who spoke English, and they never saw Americans at all; people tended to assume that I must be a Russian engineer in town to do work at the big oil refinery. But the odd thing was that there were English signs all over the place—not just the garbled "Chinglish" of restaurant menus, but road signs and billboards and gold-leaf lettering on department store windows. There was even a big sign in front of an excavation that announced in English the future home of a Walmart. I asked my friend why they did this, when she was the only person I'd met there who knew English, and she laughed and said, "We think English makes things look more modern."

She needed to be fluent in English because of her job.

She worked at the government travel agency, arranging trips to America for the locals. She said that it wasn't particularly difficult—there were only two places anybody wanted to go, Las Vegas and Atlantic City. The practical challenge was that nobody in Harbin had a credit card, and no hotel in America would let a visitor in without one. So she spent most of her day on the phone with card-issuing banks arranging temporary cards. She'd even adopted an Anglo name for herself, Jennifer—she insisted that I call her that—because she was tired of trying to teach Americans how to pronounce her real name. She'd picked it because it was the name of the heroine in the old American show *Hart to Hart*—that had been a great favorite of hers when she was a girl.

Harbin was an odd place, even by Chinese standards. It had originally been built and inhabited in the nineteenth century by Russians constructing the great Trans-Siberian Railway. The Russians were long gone but their architecture remained; the city core, meticulously preserved, was like a mirage of Saint Petersburg floating on the endless grasslands of Heilongjiang Province. But in recent years its tasteful blocks of pale European brick, with onion-dome churches for punctuation, had been surrounded by a tangle of Asian commercial modernism, as neon-lit as a set from *Blade Runner*. That afternoon, my wife and our traveling companions were shopping in the new behemoth mall, while Jennifer and I were strolling along the stately old boulevard, strewn by new-fallen leaves, that led down to the Heilong River.

Jennifer was asking me about America. I had a hard time thinking of what to tell her that wouldn't sound like a nonsensical down-market version of *Hart to Hart*. (Her only other big cultural touchstone for America was even less helpful: *Baywatch*.) That may be why I began telling her about the old family house in Edwardsville, Hilda's unhappy marriage, Helen's silent commutes into Saint Louis with her movie magazines, and the decades-long standoff between Marty and Eugene.

I couldn't tell how much of the story Jennifer understood—but then, to be fair, I wasn't sure how much of it I understood, either. It just nagged at me. Even here, it kept coming back to me. One night we had been riding on a highway in the middle of nowhere, through the pitch-black of the Heilongjiang countryside, amid a typical swarm of industrial and military traffic; we had trailed a flatbed truck carrying a stack of rubber piping for many miles, and I had watched as the tarp had blown back and one long blue pipe had slowly extruded itself and waggled at us. The highway was blasted by fierce arc lights on tall masts; snow was sifting down through the glare; I could see nothing on either side but the complicated blaze of the oil refinery on the horizon. It was as far away from my own life as I had ever gotten. And yet all I could think was that the empty depth of the night was like the Illinois countryside around Edwardsville.

"Are you going to write about your family?" Jennifer asked.

"I don't know," I answered. "I do think about it sometimes."

"I don't understand," she said. "Why wouldn't you?"

I made a vague movement of dismissal with my hand. "Oh, you know. It would be difficult, gathering up those old letters and things. It was a long time ago. The people who knew the story best, a lot of them have died. And some of the others don't want to talk about it. They'd rather just remember the best things about the house. They ask me why I want to dredge up all that unhappiness again."

"Dredge?" she asked.

I laughed, and gestured out at the river. "Like bringing things up from the bottom of the river."

She looked out over the water and said, "But you must remember the story of your family. It's important."

I didn't answer. I considered saying that I hadn't given up on it; it was like a familiar stone or weathered piece of drift glass carried in a coat pocket. I'd even gone back to Edwardsville to see whether there was anything I'd missed. But I had the feeling it was getting to be too late and too much of it had already slipped irretrievably away.

But I didn't say that to Jennifer. Instead we stood for a long while on the promenade that overlooked the river and we said nothing at all.

On our first night in Edwardsville, my wife and I had had dinner with two friends who were professors at the university.

Both specialized in regional history, and they could speak eloquently and in detail about the transformation of Edwardsville from the town I remembered to its current identity, as just one more bedroom community in the great exurban ring surrounding metropolitan Saint Louis. But the truth was, they hardly needed to say anything at all. They needed only to gesture at the restaurant around us. It was one of the most popular spots in the area, even though it was situated deep in the old farm country, with nothing around it for miles but woodland and open fields. It was mocked up to look like a traditional ranch cookhouse, with trestle tables and red-checked tablecloths; there were antique bridles and saddles draped over the varnished rafters. The food was mock-rustic as well, heavy on the chicken-fried steak and the green beans in porked vinegar; before you even ordered, a waitress set down a platter of fried chicken on the table as though it were a basket of dinner rolls. The crowd was strictly suburban, the men in horizontally striped polyester pullovers and the women in pastel stretch pants; there was a continual riot of kids in the aisles. Outside, the parking lot was jammed with station wagons and SUVs.

It was a clammy night at the beginning of winter. Once we were clear of the floodlights around the parking lot the sky resumed its old star-flecked depth, browsed here and there by flocks of moonlit clouds. The land was the same as I remembered—endless blurs of woodlands on either side of the road, opening up to disclose vistas of dreamy vagueness. But it seemed as though the vistas were more frequently lit up than they used to be by the remote spangles of subdivisions, and in the middle distance were the complicated silhouettes of radio towers, each tipped by the stately pulse of a red light. The Mississippi was shrouded in drifts of fog; past the clutter of piers, and the lights stretching out into the dark, I could see a vast shadow moving through the dimness, one of the industrial barges that dominate the river traffic now the way steamboats did in the nineteenth century.

We were staying at a bed-and-breakfast in the old river town of Alton. We had the attic room, kitted out in the style of a decorating magazine with quilts and knickknacks. It was warm in the chill night and my wife fell asleep with her usual ease, like a lion recently shot by a tranquilizer gun. I stood for a long while at the window. The town was dark, except for a few stray glows—ice-blue fluorescent in the window of a closed diner, yellow above a garage door. At long intervals, I heard a strange noise floating in from somewhere in the surrounding woodland: the mourning whistle of a train on a remote stretch of track. It had an especially forlorn sound that night, as though it were the call of a predator from inside a game reserve.

The next day we took a tour. In the morning we drove through the village of Pierron, where my family had had its first hotel and where they'd had a street named after them. The hotel was long gone, and the street signs (in the sort of garble that had long dogged the family name) now read "Schnert St." In Edwardsville there had been more erasures. Along Troy Road

I looked for the big white clapboard building that had housed Sehnert's Hotel. It had burned down a few years earlier, and there was nothing there but a grassy lot. We parked the car and meandered to the railroad tracks. There was no danger of being run over; this stretch of rail had been left derelict for years, and we could see that, several hundred yards down, there was now a work crew tearing out the track. Faint sounds of complaining metal drifted to us. A crane raised one long gleaming splinter of metal and pivoted to lay it on a waiting truck bed.

I thought about how Bosh and the other Sehnert boys had come out here at night with lanterns, and I looked for the station. It was still where it had always been, squatting beside the tracks. It was boarded up and there was a large notice on the door. I assumed it was a warning to stay out, but when we wandered closer, I saw that it was an announcement from the local historical society that they were going to attempt to move and preserve the station and needed volunteers.

The door suddenly swung open. There emerged a bustling, smiling, red-faced man in a bright red-checked coat. He immediately said hello, vigorously shook our hands, and asked whether we wanted a look inside. The interior proved to be empty of everything except a time-blackened potbellied stove in the corner.

"You folks interested in E'ville history?" our guide asked. "Or are you railroad fans?"

"My great-grandfather," I said, "was a conductor on this line. My grandfather was, too, for a while."

His face brightened in surprise. He said, "Then you're going to want to see this." He led me into a cubbyhole office next to the waiting room. It, too, had been emptied out, except for an ancient rolltop desk against the back wall. "I don't know what you can make of it," he said. "But take a look through."

He slid up the rolltop. Neatly stacked and banded on the desktop were paper slips. They were floridly printed with swirling flourishes of pastel color, and they had blanks where conductors had filled in dates and destinations. I looked through one of the stacks at random; the dates were all from 1896. "The conductors would collect them and bring them back from the runs," he said. "Maybe those are some your great-grandfather did." I looked again at the handwriting on the top slip. It was a looping scrawl in faded brown ink that read "Springfield." Could that have been Bosh's handwriting? And if it was, what could it tell me? I picked up another stack and flipped through it, seeing the names of destinations flicker past, so many journeys for so many unrecoverable purposes.

We left the station and drove down Troy Road to Second Avenue. The street was indistinguishable from any other that had been zoned for light industry. We parked at the head of the block and stood for a long while, taking in the truck lots and the chemical plant and the refinishing shop. There were faint sounds from one of the buildings, the whine and growl of some mechanical process, but I couldn't tell from which building. Nothing moved. At the far end of the block was the radio tower, looming over the street like one of the giant mechanical walkers in *The War of the Worlds*. At its peak was a red light, slowly and gravely blinking.

The house was gone. It had met the destiny recommended by the real estate developer: Bosh's acreage was now paved over for a commercial parking lot. A scattering of pickup trucks and vans stood on the asphalt behind a chain-link fence. Behind it was the line of power pylons marking out where the train tracks had once been, and beyond were a couple of garages and warehouses.

A door slammed. A man emerged from one of the buildings down the block and hurried down to the parking lot. He was wearing a white shirt, a black tie, and dark slacks; he had a crew cut and horn-rimmed glasses and he was carrying a clipboard fluttering with invoices. The whole way to his pickup truck, he had his head turned to stare at us, goggle-eyed with wonder about what our business on this street could possibly be.

Sunlight was fanning down over the river surface, lighting up a churn of brown water behind a large motorboat and a swirl of gray and brown gulls rising and scattering toward the far shore. Jennifer broke the silence. "Do you see that house?" She was pointing across the river. "That red house."

Among a cluttered row of buildings along the water's edge was a wooden house painted bright red, with a peaked roof.

"Yes, I see it," I said.

She said, "It is like your family's house, I think."

"Why do you say that?" I asked.

"When I was a child," she said, "my mother would bring me here and I would look at that house and I would imagine that one day I would visit it. I could not think of anything so happy as that, how I would cross the river to that house."

"What did you imagine was inside?" I asked.

She shrugged and shook her head. Then she smiled at me.

"Did you ever do it?" I asked.

"No," she said. "Not then. But now, yes. Many times. It is a popular restaurant." She regarded me for a long moment and then she looked back over the water. "You know that the Heilong River means in English the Black Dragon River. And Harbin means 'white bird.' But maybe you do not know the story of those names."

"No," I said.

She said, "There was a black dragon and a white dragon. The white dragon was stronger. It was an invader from the north country. The black dragon was not as strong. But it was beloved by the people here. One day the two dragons met here in a great battle in the clouds. The black dragon was wounded and it fell from the sky. It hid from the white dragon at the bottom of the river. The white dragon searched for it everywhere. But now all the white birds flew to the river to protect the black dragon. They all came together here on the water and they formed the shape of a dragon. So you see what happened? The white dragon could see the black dragon at the bottom of the river. But it saw its shape only. Because of the white birds all on the water together, he thought he was looking at his own reflection. He flew away. And so the black dragon was saved."

She paused. "That was a long time ago, of course. Since then, the dragons all went away. And then the river was polluted and all the white birds went away. And now . . ." She made a gesture taking in the river and the town. "Now you see our government cares about pollution. It is cleaning the river. The river is much cleaner now than when I was a child." She glanced over at me and smiled. She said, "But I do not think the dragons will come back. Do you?"

I shook my head.

"No," she said. "They will not. They are not real. But maybe the white birds will come back."

"That's a sad story," I said.

"Yes, very sad," she said. "All stories of the past are sad."

Acknowledgments and Thanks

An early version of *The Distancers* was published as a weekly serial in the *Chicago Reader* from April to July 2004. My first and deepest thanks must go to Alison True, the editor of the *Reader*, who encouraged me to explore my family history, gave me a remarkable amount of freedom in how to write it, and repeatedly fronted me money so I could go back to Edwardsville for research. In Edwardsville I got invaluable help from Ellen Nore Nordhauser and Norman Nordhauser of Southern Illinois University; Ellen is also coauthor, with Dick Norrish, of *Edwardsville: An Illustrated History*, a book without which mine would have been impossible.

After its initial publication I put *The Distancers* up on my website, leesandlin.com, and over the next few years extensively revised and expanded the text. For the Vintage edition I have now revised it again, to what I intend to be its final form. Major gratitude is due to Tim O'Connell, LuAnn Walther, Kathleen Cook, Russell Perrault, Angie Venezia, and everyone else involved at Vintage Books. Extra-special, extra-strength thanks must go out to my agent, Danielle Egan-Miller, whose unfailing advocacy of *The Distancers* has been gratifying, consoling, and heartening beyond what I can say.